state of world population 2003

making 1 billion count: investing in adolescents' health and rights

United Nations Population Fund
Thoraya Ahmed Obaid, Executive Director

contents

1 overview of adolescent life

Introduction

The largest generation of adolescents in history—1.2 billion strong—is preparing to enter adulthood in a rapidly changing world. Their educational and health status, their readiness to take on adult roles and responsibilities, and the support they receive from their families, communities and governments will determine their own future and the future of their countries.

Nearly half of all people are under the age of 25—the largest youth generation in history. *The State of World Population 2003* report examines the challenges and risks faced by this generation that impact directly on their physical, emotional and mental well-being. Today millions of adolescents and young people are faced with the prospects of early marriage and child-bearing, incomplete education, and the threat of HIV/AIDS. Half of all new HIV infections occur in people aged 15 to 24. The report stresses that increasing the knowledge, opportunities, choices and participation of young people will enable them to lead healthy and productive lives so that they can contribute fully to their communities and to a more stable and prosperous world.

Today's adolescents and young people have diverse experiences given the different political, economic, social and cultural realities they face in their communities. Yet there is a common thread running through all of their lives and that is the hope for a better future. This hope is bolstered by the Millennium Development Goals agreed to by world leaders in 2000 to reduce extreme poverty and hunger, slow the spread of HIV/AIDS, reduce maternal and child mortality, ensure universal primary education and improve sustainable development by 2015.

Within the framework of human rights established and accepted by the global community, certain rights are particularly relevant to adolescents and youth and the opportunities and risks they face. These include gender equality and the rights to education and health, including reproductive and sexual health information and services appropriate to their age, capacities and circumstances. Actions to ensure these rights can have tremendous practical benefits: empowering individuals, ensuring well-being, stemming the HIV/AIDS pandemic, reducing poverty and improving prospects for social and economic progress. Addressing these challenges is an urgent development priority.

Investing in young people will yield large returns for generations to come. Failing to act, on the other hand, will incur tremendous costs to individuals, societies and the world at large.

> *Investing in adolescents' health and rights will yield large benefits for generations to come.*

In every region, there is a need for positive dialogue and greater understanding among parents, families, communities and governments about the complex and sensitive situations facing adolescents and young people. The report examines such factors as changing family structures and living conditions, rapidly changing norms and social behaviours, the growth in orphans and street children, the impact of urbanization and migration, armed conflict, the lack of education and employment, and the continuing toll of gender discrimination and violence.

Just as they need guidance, young women and men need supportive relationships and institutions that respond to their hopes and concerns. By taking concerted and comprehensive action to address the challenges faced by adolescents and young people, governments can meet their commitments and international development goals, and give greater hope to the world's largest youth generation.

UNFPA, the United Nations Population Fund, is working with a wide range of partners and with young people themselves to address the needs of adolescents and young people in a way that is culturally sensitive, locally driven and in line with international human rights standards.

Adolescence is a growth process. Guiding children as they grow to adulthood is not and never has been a job for parents alone. In traditional rural communities, the extended family and established systems of hierarchy and respect govern the transition. But in all developing countries, the certainties of rural tradition are giving way to urban life, with its opportunities and risks, its individual freedoms and its more complex social demands and frameworks of support.

In the rapidly changing urban environment, young people derive most of their information about the world, what to expect and how to behave, from their peers, and increasingly from mass media. The tension between parents, who tend to see them as children in need of protection, and the outside world, which makes demands on them as adults, reflects the central dilemma of modern adolescents.

The ages from 10-19 are rich in life transitions. How and when young people experience these vary greatly depending on their circumstances. At age 10, the expectation in most societies is that children live at home, go to school, have not yet gone through puberty, are unmarried and have never worked. By their 20th birthday, many adolescents have left school and home. They have become sexually active, married and entered the labour force.[1]

While there is little comparative research, differences within and between societies are more pronounced with regard to adolescents, and generalizations may be less useful than with other age groups—some societies barely recognize a prolonged transition to adulthood; in others, adolescence seems to extend from late childhood into the 20s.

Moreover, we know far less in a systematic way about adolescents than about other age groups and even less about early adolescence, from 10 to 14, than about the later years, 15-19.

While information on young people is starting to improve,[2] there is little reliable data on the strongest influences on their lives: their peers, their families, and their communities.

Policy makers, communities and families need to create policies, programmes and guidance to give the largest number of the young the resources they need to contribute to their societies.

Why is Reproductive Health Important?

Sexual and reproductive health has been defined by the international community as a state of complete physical, mental, and social well being, and not just merely the absence of disease or infirmity, in all matters relating to the reproductive system and to its functions and processes.[3] It is an essential component of young people's ability to become well-adjusted, responsible and productive members of society.[4]

Subsequent chapters of this report detail the major issues involved in ensuring adolescents' rights and meeting their needs in relation to sexual and reproductive health.

Figure 1: Adolescent Population by Region, 2003 and 2050

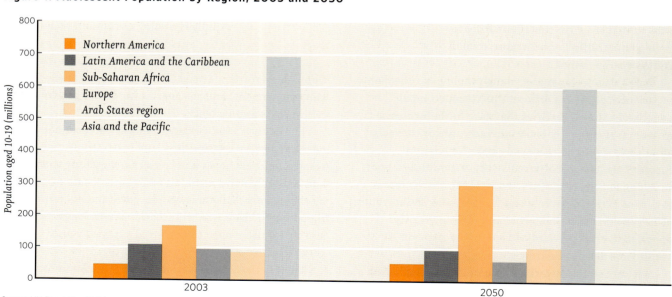

Source: UN Population Division

Chapter 2 examines gender inequality in relation to early marriage, premarital sexual activity and violence against women and girls. Chapter 3 looks at HIV/AIDS and its impact on the young. Chapter 4 highlights efforts to influence adolescents' behaviour by giving them information about sexual and reproductive health. Chapter 5 discusses the provision of "youth-friendly" reproductive health services. Chapter 6 gives examples of comprehensive programmes addressing adolescents' needs for information, services and skills training. Finally, Chapter 7 outlines necessary policy changes and benefits of investing in adolescents, including their sexual and reproductive health.

Reproductive health is a lifelong concern. A mother's reproductive health status has an impact on her children and their health.

As boys and girls grow up, adults treat them differently and establish different expectations for their behaviour. The differences often determine life outcomes, and many are related to or have an impact on sexuality. In a wide variety of social settings, overtly or by insinuation, girls are conditioned from childhood to expect the role of wife and mother, and boys to expect the role of breadwinner and head of household. Demands on children exist inside the home and out of it; whether children can expect education and in what form; the teenager's introduction to sexuality, courtship and marriage practices; and information and services regarding reproductive health before and during marriage, reflect these differential gender expectations.

Adverse reproductive health outcomes in later adolescence, including unwanted pregnancy, unsafe abortion and sexually transmitted infections (STIs), can be ascribed to conditions such as lack of education and opportunity, but occur in all social groups. Often, differential gender expectations and treatment in childhood and the early teenage years are important contributors.

Expectations that young women should be responsible for contraception, pressure on young men to prove their masculinity, the aggressive/submissive behaviour exhibited by many young people, for example, are the outcomes of behaviour patterns established early in life.

These matters are often difficult to discuss and hard for young people themselves to raise. Part of the reason, or at least the rationale, for public reticence is that young people themselves do not put sexual and reproductive health high on their list of active concerns. But reproductive health is connected to many of their top-line issues, such as completing education, finding employment, securing their economic position, making secure relationships and, eventually, founding a family of their own.

> **I** | **DEFINING THE YOUNG** The terms "adolescents", "youth" and "young people" are used differently in various societies. These categories are associated—where they are recognized at all—with different roles, responsibilities and ages that depend on the local context.
>
> As this report details, key life events—marriage, sexual debut (first sexual intercourse), employment, childbearing, acceptance into adult organizations, political participation—occur at differing times between and within societies.
>
> This report uses definitions that are commonly used in different demographic, policy and social contexts:
>
> - **Adolescents**: 10-19 years of age (early adolescence, 10-14; late adolescence, 15-19).
> - **Youth**: 15-24 years of age.
> - **Young people**: 10-24 years of age.
>
> National programmes and policies often make different distinctions. In India, for example, the Youth Policy includes people up to the age of 35. In Jamaica, reproductive health programmes for adolescents have different goals and strategies for differing ages (recognizing that the interests, skills and needs of younger adolescents are not the same as those of the older). In many countries, health education materials are tailored to different grade levels.

Teachers, spiritual leaders, employers, governments and communities must help young people, and their parents, as they prepare to exercise the rights and responsibilities of adulthood. Political systems must find ways to involve young people in making and executing the policies that shape their lives. The remainder of this chapter provides a glimpse into the range of situations that must be addressed.

Adolescent Reproductive Health and Poverty

Reducing poverty requires progress in addressing adolescent reproductive health needs.

Education is a key for breaking the transmission of poverty from one generation to the next. Yet studies show that the poor are more likely to not complete schooling.[5] Consequently, they are deprived of the education on reproductive health and sexuality that is provided at higher grade levels and do not know how to find health information.

Poorer young women are likely to marry earlier.[6] In the wealthiest 20 per cent of the population, marriage before age 18 is relatively rare (less than 30 per cent, in countries where the national average exceeds 50 per cent).

In Nigeria, almost 80 per cent of the poorest young women marry before age 18 while only 22 per cent of the richest do.

Differences in adolescent fertility are driven by many factors, including life opportunities, service access, provider attitudes, sociocultural expectations, gender inequalities, educational aspirations and economic levels. Fertility differences between the poorest and richest strata in many countries are among the largest of any health indicator.[7] Early childbearing in poor families perpetuates an intergenerational cycle of poverty.

Modern contraceptive use among adolescents is generally low, but increases with economic status. Fewer than 5 per cent of the poorest young use modern contraception. Inequities in access to family planning increase the likelihood of unwanted or ill-timed births. (See Chapter 2).

Poorer young women are less likely to have their births attended by a skilled health worker. The richest young women are two to eight times more likely to have their births attended by a medical professional. Skilled attendance is important for the health of the mother and the child, particularly when there are delivery complications. The younger the mother, the greater the chance that she will face complications during pregnancy and childbirth. Also, those who are poor have the least access to health care services to deal with increased pregnancy and delivery risks.

HIV/AIDS is a disease associated with poverty. Poor women are least able to negotiate safer sex and more likely to accept partners with hopes of material benefit. This social vulnerability is compounded by a lack of information. Poor women are less likely to know that HIV/AIDS is sexually transmitted.

POVERTY AND ECONOMIC GROWTH The number of youth in the world surviving on less than a dollar a day in 2000 was an estimated 238 million, almost a quarter (22.5 per cent) of the world's total youth population.[8] About 462 million young people live on less than $2 a day. South Asia has the largest concentration of young people in extreme poverty (106 million) followed by sub-Saharan Africa (60 million), East Asia and the Pacific (51 million) and Latin America and the Caribbean (15 million).

Eleven large countries account for 77 per cent of the 238 million young people living in extreme poverty—India, China, Nigeria, Pakistan, Bangladesh, the Democratic Republic of Congo, Viet Nam, Brazil, Ethiopia, Indonesia and Mexico. Youth poverty also correlates closely with national indebtedness.

AN OPPORTUNITY While population growth and persistent poverty in developing countries are linked in a vicious cycle, the large number of young people alive today presents a unique economic opportunity. As fertility

---

2 **REPRODUCTIVE HEALTH IS A HUMAN RIGHT** In 1994, the International Conference on Population and Development (ICPD) stressed the importance of adolescence to sexual and reproductive health throughout the life cycle. It also—for the first time in an international agreement—recognized that adolescents have particular health needs that differ in important ways from those of adults, and stressed that gender equity is an essential component of efforts to meet those needs.

The ICPD Programme of Action urges governments and health systems to establish, expand or adjust programmes to meet adolescents' reproductive and sexual health needs, to respect rights to privacy and confidentiality, and to ensure that attitudes of health care providers do not restrict adolescents' access to information and services. It further urges governments to remove any barriers (laws, regulations or social customs) between adolescents and reproductive health information, education, and services.

The 1999 Special Session of the General Assembly, ICPD+5, recognized the right of adolescents to the highest attainable standards of health, and provision of appropriate, specific, user-friendly and accessible services to address effectively their reproductive and sexual health needs including reproductive health education, information, counselling and health promotion strategies [paragraph 73].

Article 24 of the Convention on the Rights of the Child affirms that children have the right to attain the highest standards of health and to health care, including family planning education and services (a right also recognized in earlier conventions and conferences).

In June 2003, the UN committee that monitors the implementation of the Convention elaborated: "States Parties should provide adolescents with access to sexual and reproductive information, including on family planning and contraceptives, the dangers of early pregnancy, the prevention of HIV/AIDS and prevention and treatment of STIs. In addition, States Parties should ensure access to appropriate information regardless of marital status, and prior consent from parents or guardians."

The Convention on the Elimination of All Forms of Discrimination against Women (1979) supports women's rights to reproductive health information and services and to equity in reproductive decision-making and matters of sexual health. In 1999, the committee that oversees the implementation of this treaty urged state signatories to accept that whenever the Convention uses the term "women" it applies to girls and female adolescents as well.

rates decline, the proportion of the population of working age (15 to 60) increases relative to that of "dependent" ages (0 to 15 and 60 and over). This opens a "demographic window".[9] With appropriate investments in health and education and conducive economic policies and governance, countries can mobilize their young people's potential, and launch an economic and social transformation. The demographic window will close as populations age and dependency increases once more.

Countries like Thailand and the Republic of Korea have already taken advantage of their "demographic window" by investing in social programmes to secure dramatic economic growth. The window is now opening for a large group of countries where fertility has declined sharply in the last two decades. For the least developed countries, with the highest fertility and slowest declines, the window will not open until after 2050 (Figure 1).[10]

Opportunities vary considerably within countries; levels of dependency are highest in poor families, where fertility levels are highest.[11] Persistent high fertility in poor households undermines the prospects for development. Taking advantage of the demographic window calls for investments in health (including reproductive health) and education for the poorest families.

In many regions and countries it will be the adolescents of today who will be part of the working age population when the demographic bonus reaches its peak.

Investing in their health, education and skills and establishing a supportive policy framework for economic and social growth should be a critical priority. In the least developed countries, even greater investments will be needed to improve the quality of life and governance and accelerate the demographic transition—opening the window of opportunity wider and earlier.

A Changing World

Adolescents are inheriting a rapidly changing world increasingly shaped by global influences, among them:

- Globalization of trade, investment and economic relationships.

- Mass communications media and the development of a youth culture.

- Modes of governance and exclusion of certain social groups.

- Decentralization of decision-making.

- Changing nature of work, requiring new skills and capacities.

- Urbanization and migration.

- Emerging and resurgent diseases, particularly HIV/AIDS.

---

3 **POPULATION GROWTH IS SLOWING BUT STILL HIGH IN THE POOREST COUNTRIES** Lower fertility and higher than expected AIDS-related mortality are combining to slow global population growth, according to the latest UN projections. But *World Population Prospects: The 2002 Revision* shows that population is still growing rapidly in the world's poorest countries.

Now 6.3 billion, world population will grow to an estimated 8.9 billion people by 2050. Nearly all of the 2.6 billion increase will be in the developing countries of Africa, Asia and Latin America.

The United Nations Population Division revises its projections every two years, and the 2002 projection for 2050 is lower by 400 million than the one made in 2000. An increase in projected AIDS-related deaths (278 million by 2050) account for half of the revision; the rest is the result of lower fertility and smaller family size.

The UN report shows that investment in reproductive health programmes, including family planning, has helped reduce fertility in developing countries from six children per woman in 1960 to around three today. Further declines in fertility are contingent on the ability of couples worldwide to realize their desire for smaller families.

Continued investment is critical. The Population Division notes that if women have, on average, half a child more than its "most likely" projection scenario, world population could rise to 10.6 billion by 2050.

The unprecedented number of adolescents alive today—1.2 billion, a reflection of high fertility a generation ago—will ensure continued population growth for decades even as families get smaller. While adolescents' share of the total population will decrease over time,

their total numbers will stay within the range of 1.2 to 1.3 billion throughout the next 50 years. Enabling young women to postpone childbearing and to space births more widely is therefore key to slowing the momentum of population growth.

Growth rates and fertility are falling much more slowly in the poorest countries than elsewhere. The 49 least developed countries are expected to grow from 668 million people today to 1.7 billion by 2050, and their share of the world's adolescent population will increase from 14 to 25.6 per cent. Sub-Saharan Africa's share will grow from 14 to 24.6 per cent.

The higher projection of AIDS-related deaths results from a more thorough assessment of the epidemic's severity in individual countries, and underscores the urgent need for increased spending on HIV/AIDS prevention and treatment.

Figure 2: Peak of Demographic Window of Opportunity, Selected Regions

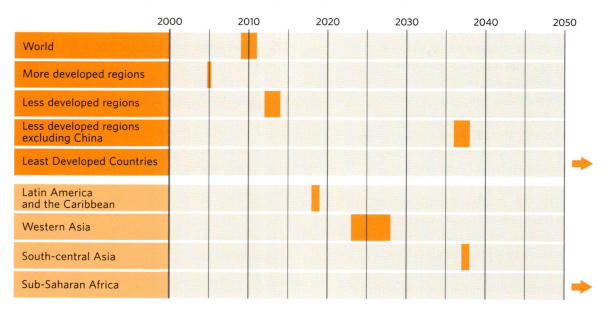

- Changing family structures and dispersal of family members.
- Trafficking in illicit drugs and human trafficking.
- Conflict and social disruption.

Political, social and economic changes and resulting social problems are affecting parent-child relationships, views of parental authority and the institutions that serve adolescents. There is great diversity in the circumstances of young people between and within countries. Some of these dimensions are addressed below.

CHANGING FAMILIES AND LIVING CONDITIONS In many settings, child-parent relationships have traditionally been just one component of a web of extended family relations. But migration, new values and understandings, poverty, family dispersal and the impacts of HIV/AIDS have reduced reliance on the extended family, particularly in cities. This has increased demands on parents while depriving them of systems of support.

Many young people are living without one or both of their parents, and may not be able to rely on their families for support. An analysis of survey data for selected countries in the late 1990s[12] shows the proportions of young adolescents aged 10-14 not living with either parent ranged from less than 3 per cent in Jordan and 13 per cent in Nicaragua to more than 20 per cent in some African countries, and that more girls than boys were in this

situation. Those living with one parent (more often the mother than the father in most countries) ranged from less than 10 per cent in Jordan to 32 per cent in Nicaragua. While data on urban-rural differences are scarce, in Ethiopia 60 per cent of rural young adolescents shared living quarters with both parents compared to 41 per cent of urban girls and 47 per cent of boys.

ORPHANS AND STREET CHILDREN The loss of one or both parents dramatically changes adolescents' lives, forcing them to become heads of households or onto the streets. Poverty and political and ethnic conflict exacerbate the situation.

AIDS has so far orphaned at least 13 million children currently under the age of 15. The total number of children orphaned by the epidemic since it began is forecast to more than double by 2010.[13] Before the onset of AIDS, about 2 per cent of children in developing countries were orphans. Today, in 10 countries of sub-Saharan Africa—Botswana, Burundi, Central African Republic, Lesotho, Malawi, Mozambique, Rwanda, Swaziland, Zambia and Zimbabwe—more than 15 per cent of children under age 15 have been orphaned.[14]

There are many other reasons for adolescents to seek refuge in the streets. Homes and families disintegrate through war or civil emergency.[15] Children may be driven out by extreme poverty, violence or substance abuse in the family, or conflict with their relatives. They may be escaping physical or mental abuse, failure at school, mental health or behavioural problems, boredom, lack of opportunity or unsatisfactory peer relations.[16]

Global estimates of street children vary from 100 million, with half of them in Latin America,[17] to 250 million.[18] Their numbers are rapidly increasing, and more younger children are on the street than ever before.[19]

In the Philippines, for example, 220,859 street children were reported in 1991 and 1.5 million in 1999.[20] In developing countries, street children may be as young as 8, while in developed countries they tend to be over age 12.[21] Asian street children are much more likely to be male than female. Girls are less visible on the streets, possibly because fewer girls leave or are abandoned by their families; or because girls are picked up more rapidly by authorities or are confined and exploited.

Because of their precarious residential and economic circumstances and lack of access to social service institutions, homeless young people are often malnourished, in poor health, addicted to drugs, and susceptible to sexual abuse and HIV/AIDS.[22] Generally considered "too old" to adopt, homeless adolescents are among the most neglected subgroups where any rehabilitation effort or HIV strategy is concerned.[23] Often seen as a menace to order, street youth are targets of violence by law enforcement and vigilantes alike.

URBANIZATION AND MIGRATION Rural areas are changing, small towns are becoming cities and big cities are still expanding. Urbanization is an especially important influence in the least developed countries. People migrate in response to opportunity, economic deprivation or environmental emergency, reflecting both under-investment in rural development and poor resource management.[24]

Table 1: Percentage of Adolescents Living in Cities, by Sex and Age, Selected Countries

	Girls		Boys	
	10-14	15-19	10-14	15-19
Chad (1996-1997)	22	23	23	29
Togo (1998)	34	44	28	34
Bolivia (1998)	61	75	60	69
Nicaragua (1998)	58	62	55	60
Philippines (1998)	45	57	45	51
Kyrgyzstan (1997)	26	29	25	26

Source: The Population Council

---

4 **WORKING WITH STREET YOUTH** The group *El Caracol* (The Snail) in Mexico works with street youth aged 15-23. Street educators build relationships with the young people; make presentations on HIV/AIDS, drug use and other health and social issues; and then work with the young people to identify their own needs. *El Caracol* runs a restaurant, a print shop and a rabbit farm, where street youth work as interns and apprentices. A transitional living programme provides considerable freedom and responsibility. Staff work with young people to construct new identities, helping them to shed the self-definition as "street kids."

In Nepal, the Child Welfare Scheme works in the slum areas of Pokhara and provides street youth with a health clinic and a vocational training and reintegration centre. It started in 2002 with former drug addicts and trafficked girls. Students receive three years of vocational training, and also study mathematics, science, English and Nepali. The programme builds self-esteem, offers training in first aid and social welfare to make street youth independent, and provides ongoing counselling for youths with psychological scars.

The urban experience simultaneously offers young people opportunity and exposes them to risks. In every area of their lives, migrant adolescents remain a highly vulnerable and often hard-to-reach group.

Young people may move with their families or on their own, in search of work or education. Information on why adolescents migrate is very thin and much has to be inferred from other data. Data from Togo in 1998, for example, show that 34 per cent of girls aged 10-14 lived in cities, compared to 28 per cent of boys, and that the difference increased for those aged 15-19—44 per cent of girls and 34 per cent of boys.[25] This suggests that Togo's cities offer—or seem to offer—better educational or economic opportunities for girls (Table 1). Similar patterns are seen in Bolivia and the Philippines.

The experience of rural-to-urban migrants varies considerably. In many developing countries, domestic work is one of the main sources of income for girls and young women in urban areas. In Bangladesh, textile work in cities has offered young women migrants unprecedented opportunities to earn money, save for dowries and postpone marriage; most of their experience has been very positive.[26] In Nigeria, in contrast, young women apprenticing to be tailors are very vulnerable to sexual abuse because of their subordinate position at work and separation from their families.[27]

Young women frequently migrate to cities or abroad to live with their husbands' families. This may not be a free choice, especially if the woman is poor or orphaned.[28]

In Thailand, 15-19 year olds make up the largest proportion of migrants; they report facing difficulties in the cities, and have few adults who can assist them with their problems.[29]

A study of international migrants returning to Mexico from the United States (where an estimated 8 million Mexicans work) found that 24 per cent were under age 25.[30] Eighty per cent of these young people found work in the United States, nearly all of those aged 12-17 in industry or services.

CHILDREN AND WAR Conflicts in the 1990s killed nearly 2 million children. Six million were seriously injured or permanently disabled.[31] In 2000, an estimated 300,000 child soldiers were involved in 30 conflicts around the world.[32]

Each day, 5,000 children become refugees, and one in every 230 persons in the world is a child or adolescent who has been forced to flee his or her home.[33] After more than two decades of war in Afghanistan, hundreds of thousands of adolescents are refugees in Pakistan; family poverty and a lack of access to education have led these young people to work as carpet weavers, garbage pickers, brick makers, house servants and even drug sellers.[34]

In 1998, in the Democratic Republic of Congo and in Afghanistan, children as young as 13 years of age were forcibly recruited by military forces.[35] In 1999, groups of young men were rounded up from street markets by the Angolan armed forces. In Myanmar, the army is reported to have forcibly recruited underage children from schools. In El Salvador, Ethiopia and Uganda, a third of all child soldiers were girls.

Education and Employment

Education and employment opportunities have direct and important indirect impacts on life quality, including health, and prospects for development. They are particularly important for adolescent girls' sexual and reproductive health and rights. Both allow girls and young women to gain knowledge, self-understanding, self-esteem and skills, and to earn an income. They also offer a chance to develop relationships with peers and adults outside their families, potentially important sources of information[36] that can open up new opportunities beyond early marriage and childbearing.

SCHOOLING AND GENDER DISPARITIES Most young people have some access to schooling opportunities, but the picture is very mixed: 115 million children currently do not attend primary school, 57 per cent of them girls;[37] and 57 million young men and 96 million young women aged 15-24 in developing countries cannot read or write.[38]

---

5 **SIERRA LEONE: POST-WAR RECONSTRUCTION AND ADOLESCENTS**

Several years after Sierra Leone's civil war, countless youths and adolescents, particularly girls, are still impoverished, orphaned and often sexually exploited while being excluded from reconstruction efforts, according to a 2002 research study in which the Women's Commission for Refugee Women and Children relied on adolescents as the principal researchers and respondents.

During the conflict, which ended in 1999, youth fighting for opposing sides became both perpetrators and victims of violence. Warlords promised a portion of Sierra Leone's diamond resources to youth that enlisted in the military cause, but denied the adolescent soldiers their promised payment and continuously violated their human rights. As post-war reconstruction began, adolescents were excluded from policy-making efforts, leaving them unemployed, uneducated, and without access to medical attention.

Sierra Leone lacks health clinics that are affordable and adolescent-friendly, and health education remains unattainable to most. Many youths express disbelief in sexually transmitted infections, including HIV/AIDS.

Many orphaned adolescents are involved in crime, drug use and street life. Girls and young women are often forced into early marriage or turn to sex work due to economic or parental pressure, further subjecting them to physical, mental, and sexual trauma—and the risk of contracting STIs including HIV/AIDS—as they were during the war, when rape was widespread. Recent initiatives to counter gender-based violence have not been implemented or enforced.

The combination of adolescents' distrust of adults and government, and the adults' exclusion of young people in reconstruction efforts has hindered the process of integration and peace maintenance.

A variety of children's welfare agencies offer assistance to Sierra Leone's reconstruction and to protect children's rights, but support is fragmented and there is often competition for aid packages directed to vulnerable groups. Multiple government departments handling different aspects of ensuring children's welfare lack coordination. Youth organizations lack the resources to move into policy-making.

The youth-led study recommends changes in national policies and legal frameworks to better protect children, adolescents and youth, while involving young people in policy-making, implementation, and enforcement. Citing adolescents' primary concern as the lack of education, it calls for more attention to education and vocational training. Gender equality and reproductive health are essential, it stresses, urging action to reduce sexual and physical violence and provide educational opportunities for women.

Figure 3: Percentage of Women Giving Birth by Age 20, by Level of Education

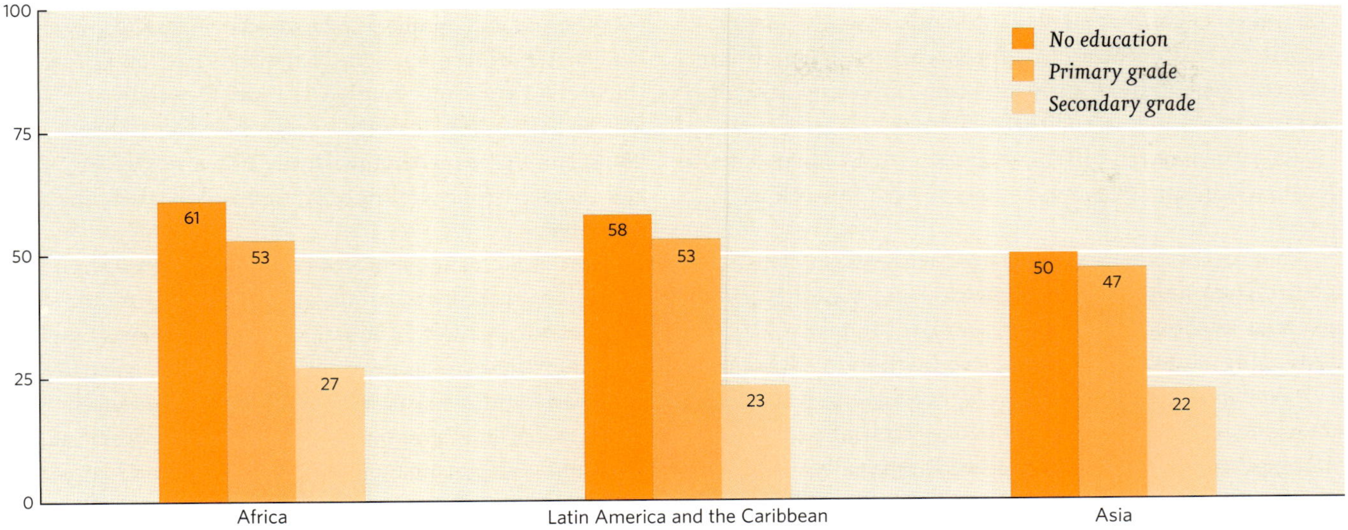

Legend:
- No education
- Primary grade
- Secondary grade

Africa: No education 61, Primary grade 53, Secondary grade 27
Latin America and the Caribbean: No education 58, Primary grade 53, Secondary grade 23
Asia: No education 50, Primary grade 47, Secondary grade 22

Source: UN Population Division

Illiteracy excludes young people from a wide range of opportunities.

There is some good news, however. According to UNESCO, girls and women in all regions are gaining access to education, closing the gap with boys and men.[39] The United Nations Girls' Education Initiative (UNGEI), launched in April 2000, seeks to accelerate educational advance by coordinating and focusing the financial and non-financial resources of multiple organizations, including governments, NGOs, and UN agencies to create a large advocacy campaign for girls' education and providing support to countries that request assistance. About 90 countries are on track to meet global goals for ending gender inequality in primary education by 2015.[40]

However, the numbers out of school increase in times of conflict, social crisis and natural disasters.[41] Gaps in post-primary education have declined but remain significant in many poor countries. In some countries boys' dropout rates exceed girls' and boys' enrolment has declined. Economic reversals and stagnation can impede progress.

In many developing countries, fewer than half of all children continue as far as secondary school. Education statistics show a sharp drop-off in girls' attendance after primary school.[42] By age 18, girls have received on average 4.4 years less education than boys.[43]

Teachers may be unwittingly or consciously contributing to the problem. Research in Kenya, for example, has shown that teachers undermine girls in the classroom, contributing to girls' feelings that they do not belong in school.[44] Teachers tolerate boys' bullying of girls and have lower expectations about girls' academic performance. Some teachers acknowledge that they preferred boys, and they often allot girls menial chores such as sweeping the classroom, while giving teaching-related tasks to boys.

Girls' are often withdrawn from school, kept at home, and generally have their interactions much more closely regulated at the onset of menstruation, or menarche.[45] Data directly linking menarche with leaving school are hard to come by, but the anthropological evidence is ample. From South India to Mexico to Egypt, girls are kept under close supervision and their mobility restricted, to a significant extent because they are seen to be vulnerable to premarital pregnancy, which goes against social norms.[46]

An early age at first marriage and childbirth is more common among women with less education.[47]

Fertility decreases with educational attainment. The largest differentials within regions are in Africa, Western Asia, and Latin America and the Caribbean, where women with secondary or higher education ultimately have three fewer children on average than those with no education. As overall family size declines, these differences become less apparent.

YOUNG PEOPLE AND EMPLOYMENT Worldwide, an estimated 352 million children between ages 5 and 17 were economically active in 2000, over 246 million of them working illegally and nearly 171 million in hazardous conditions.[48]

Despite laws against child labour, about 186 million children under age 15 were working in 2000;[49] this included 138 million children between 10 and 14—about one in four—mostly performing non-agricultural work.[50] Asia has the highest number of under-15 workers, 127.3 million, followed by 48 million in sub-Saharan Africa and 17.4 million in Latin America and the Caribbean.[51]

An estimated 141 million or 42 per cent of adolescents between the ages of 15 and 17 were engaged in work in 2000.[52]

Youth unemployment rates are high—56 per cent in South Africa, 34 per cent in Jamaica—and almost everywhere at least double the adult average.[53] In many developing countries, gender discrimination in education and job opportunities results in higher unemployment among young women.[54] Lack of education limits many young people's employment prospects, especially women's, to poorly paid and often unsafe work as domestic servants, agricultural labourers or factory workers.

Table 2: Per Cent of Adolescents Employed in 2000, by Age, Sex and Region

Region	Girls		Boys	
	10-14	15-19	10-14	15-19
Eastern Africa	35	62	38	66
Middle Africa	26	53	29	60
Northern Africa	6	21	11	41
Southern Africa	2	35	3	40
Western Africa	21	44	31	60
Caribbean	7	23	13	39
Central America	4	30	9	54
South America	7	34	11	55
Eastern Asia	0	49	7	51
South-eastern Asia	9	43	10	47
South-central Asia	13	35	14	52
Western Asia	4	25	5	41
Australia-New Zealand	0	52	0	53
Europe—Total	0	25	0	30
Western Europe	0	23	0	27
Southern Europe	0	23	0	29
Northern Europe	0	41	0	44
Eastern Europe	0	23	0	27
Melanesia	13	49	17	59
Northern America	0	38	0	41

Source: International Labour Organization

COMBINING WORK AND EDUCATION Of the economically active children and adolescents, half work full-time and half combine work with school.[56] Many young people see work less as an obstacle to education or a risk to their health and safety than a positive survival strategy for themselves and their families, a route to resources for the future and an entry to responsible adulthood. Work can provide women with their own resources and increase their choices of timing and partners in marriage.

Research on the impact of combining work and education on future earnings and life opportunities is quite scarce. A study in Brazil found mixed effects. An early start to some occupations, such as civil construction, handicrafts or commercial activities, enhanced young men's long-term prospects, but an early start usually reduced future income, primarily because work interfered with education. There were some benefits for girls in domestic employment, but their opportunities were much more limited.[57] As the skills needed for higher paid employment become more demanding, the tradeoffs may become more difficult. Further, young women who start working in adolescence have more children later.[58]

Another policy concern emerges from the large number of adolescents who are not working, in school or married. The circumstances of these young men and women are hard to discover and they are difficult to reach. In Pakistan, for example, around 12 per cent of boys aged 10 to 14 are in none of these roles and this increases to 15 per cent among those aged 15 to 19. Among girls, 30 per cent of 10-14 year olds and over 45 per cent of 15-19 year olds are "doing nothing".[59]

Ensuring a Better Future: Investment in Youth

The involvement of adolescents in social development is a task most countries have yet to address. Broad social changes are increasing the time between physical maturity and acceptance into adult social roles. Social institutions must adjust to offer adolescents full participation because in many settings, they have proven to be dynamic agents of change.

Adolescence can be neither denied nor seen as "a time between". The choices young people make, the goals they set and the opportunities they are offered are not just preparatory: they are a meaningful and important part of their lives. Young people's choices can set them on courses that can benefit or harm them, their families, friends and communities. Yet adolescents are offered inadequate information, opportunities, resources and support necessary to guide their choices.

Table 3: Consequences of Under-investment in Adolescents

Consequences of Limited Investments in Adolescent Reproductive Health & Reproductive and Development Rights

Reproductive Health Consequence	Contributing Factors	Consequences for Self	Consequences for Families, Society and National Development
Early pregnancy & childbearing	• Early marriage • Poverty (motivates early pregnancy/early marriage for economic and personal security) • Gender discrimination/low value of girls/sense of identity and control/status based on roles as wives, mothers; low self-esteem • Lack of information, education, counselling and services for prevention; lack of information about pregnancy risks at too young an age • Inability to negotiate contraceptive use, fertility decisions, or postponement of pregnancy due to gender and age, sociocultural expectations • Lack of reproductive rights	• Risks of complications from pregnancy (obstructed labour, obstetric fistulas, anaemia/haemorrhage, death) • School drop out • Diminished employment and income-earning options • Poverty • Responsibilities, pressures of childrearing too much, too soon before socio-economic and psychological development • Potential for self-development curtailed	• **Higher infant and maternal morbidity and mortality** • Higher health care costs • Higher social welfare costs, especially in the case of single and unmarried mothers • Abandonment of newborns • **Reduced prospects of eradicating poverty** (as educational level of mother is key factor in breaking intergenerational transmission of poverty) • **Reduced skilled human capital for socio-economic development; less skilled workforce; reduced earnings** • Increased dependency of young mothers on male providers (even if abusive), related to persistent gender inequality and lack of women's empowerment • Increased population momentum; **reduced demographic bonus**
Unwanted pregnancy	• Lack of reproductive rights • Low access to contraceptive information, education, counselling and services. • Myths and misconceptions about pregnancy and contraceptive safety • Gender relations—'pregnancy is woman's responsibility'; attitudes of lack of male responsibility for pregnancy prevention or consequences; gender stereotypes—girls not equipped with negotiating and assertiveness skills; submissiveness and ignorance expected of girls • Sexual violence • Forced sex and forced pregnancy as weapons of war • Poverty (less years of school, or more years out-of-school; less access to information or services, or to sexuality education; girls less informed about their bodies)	• Recourse to abortion, including unsafe abortion (with high risks of maternal morbidity or death) • Single and early motherhood • Larger family size than the partners desire • Reduced chances for self-development and skills-building to break out of poverty	• **Reduced investments in children's needs and development** • **Reinforcement of gender inequality—loss of socio-economic opportunities and women's full development potential** • Increased population momentum

Consequences of Limited Investments in Adolescent Reproductive Health & Reproductive and Development Rights

Reproductive Health Consequence	Contributing Factors	Consequences for Self	Consequences for Families, Society and National Development
Sexual Abuse, Violence & Exploitation	• Children and adolescents, especially girls, subject to sexual abuse and incest – silence kept from fear, lack of education, marginalization, lack of protection, and social norms and taboos • Poverty (false promises of increased income for self and family) • Sexual trafficking and slavery profitable; limited enforcement, corruption, etc.; lack of protections for at-risk or already enslaved girls • Conflict and post-conflict situations (increased sexual abuse and rape because of fragmented social and family fabric) • Low status of girls and young women; low self-esteem; male power and sociocultural legitimacy of sexual violence	• Psychological, physical and emotional trauma • Unwanted pregnancy, unsafe abortion, STIs/HIV/AIDS • Impaired ability to establish trusting relations, intimacy, sexual relations; increased prospects of repetitively abusive relationships • Reduced freedom, life in fear and violence, including freedom of movement	• Persistence of gender violence and sexual abuse of children and adolescents (violating universal values and human rights related to respect for human dignity, personal and bodily integrity, freedom and self-determination, and fundamental reproductive rights) • Reinforcement of acceptability of violence • Diminished educational attainment; increased absenteeism from work and reduced productivity and loss of income to employers • Increased crime, reduced law and order, increased corruption (from sexual trafficking) • Depression • **Slowed progress against HIV/AIDS**
STIs/ HIV/AIDS	• Lack of information on safer sex • Gender discrimination/lack of decision-making power • Lack of access to methods of protection • Sexual abuse, violence and exploitation • Poverty (leads to transactional or intergenerational sex) • Multiple sexual partners	• Premature death or potential self-development curtailed • Discrimination and stigma • Increased poverty • Infertility • Cervical cancer and other sequelae of some non-fatal infections • Orphanhood	• Lost productivity and investments • Hopelessness and anomie • Agricultural, health, education and other systems fail • **Disruption of social and economic systems** • Overburden of health care system • Destruction of family networks
Under-employment	• Weak job creation • Low entrepreneurial skills • Socio-economic exclusion • Gender discrimination in employment and remuneration and unrecognized labour	• Lack of skills • Unsafe exploitation • Child labour, and sexual exploitation, Transactional sex • Poverty	• National stability and security harmed • **Economic growth and social development reduced** • Increased marginalization • Low social mobility • Poor health, nutrition and education
Low civil and social participation	• Lack of settings/institutions for including young people • Restrictions on girls' mobility and gender segregation • Social and political exclusion	• Lack of opportunities to participate and voice concerns • Inability to use democratic institutions	• Disenfranchised youth as a source of civil unrest • Lack of inputs from young people in the development of policies and programmes • Lack of social and political tolerance

Note: Points presented in bold type reflect issues addressed in the Millennium Development Goals

In many cases, legal frameworks and administrative arrangements exist to provide young people with essential services such as employment guidance, education and health care, including reproductive health information and services. The problem is more often one of the implementation of policy than of making it.

Investments in adolescents must be strategic. The returns will be generous (see Chapter 7). Inadequate investment stifles opportunity and exposes young people to unnecessary risks. Different sorts of deprivation reinforce each other.

However, investing in young people's health, education and employment; promoting their social and political inclusion; and reducing the risks to which they are exposed also has a reinforcing effect and promotes a wide spectrum of human rights and development goals. This is certainly true of investments to prevent early marriage and to help adolescents avoid early and unwanted pregnancy, coerced sex, unsafe motherhood and sexually transmitted infections including HIV/AIDS.

This report provides examples of strategies that work, a starting point for reflection, adaptation and improvement.

---

6 **RECOGNIZING ADOLESCENTS' 'EVOLVING CAPACITIES'** The Convention on the Rights of the Child details governments' responsibility to guarantee the rights of all children up to age 18, including the right to privacy (Article 16), and to information "regardless of frontiers" (Article 13). All but three countries (the United States, Timor-Leste and Somalia) have adopted the Convention.

The Convention also acknowledges that children's ability to make important decisions, including decisions about their health, increases with age and experience.

Article 5 calls on governments to respect the rights and duties of parents, legal guardians and extended families or communities (if empowered by local custom) to guide and direct children in the exercise of their rights "in a manner consistent with the evolving capacities of the child".

The ICPD similarly noted the need to balance the responsibilities and rights of parents or guardians with the "evolving capacities" of "adolescents" (a term not in the Convention but used throughout the ICPD Programme of Action).

"Children incapable of judgement [Note: this is a legal term for incapacity or lack of maturity] are entitled to the protection and guidance that parents or guardians can provide," say legal scholars Rebecca Cook and Bernard Dickens. But the concept of "evolving capacities" also implies increasing autonomy. Policies "that treat competent adults as if they are children," they argue, "can become demeaning and insulting." Laws ostensibly designed to protect adolescents, for example by denying them access to contraception without parental consent, can jeopardize their health and may also violate the Convention and other human rights treaties.

2 gender inequality and reproductive health

For many millions of young people, adolescence is now a critical passage in which they gain life experience through schooling, job training, work experiences, community activities, youth groups and relationships. A majority also have their first sexual experiences during the adolescent years.

Adolescents also learn the social and gender norms that prevail in their communities; some protect their health and rights, and some do not. These norms confront girls with special challenges—including restrictions on their independence and mobility, inequality in educational and employment opportunities, pressure to marry and start bearing children at an early age, and unequal power relations that limit their control over their sexual and reproductive lives.

DISCRIMINATION IS PERVASIVE Throughout much of the world, families and societies treat girls and boys unequally, with girls disproportionately facing privation, lack of opportunity and lower levels of investment in their health,[1] nutrition[2] and education.[3] Gender-based discrimination continues in adolescence and is often a constant feature of adulthood.

Prevailing gender norms also stymie adolescent girls' access to schooling and employment opportunities. Institutionalized legal inequality underpins laws that keep land, money and other economic resources out of girls' and women's hands,[4] closing off avenues for redress of discrimination and creating the conditions for gender-based violence and exploitation.[5]

Unequal power relations between females and males lead to widespread violations of health and human rights. Among the most persistent and pernicious are early or child marriage, sexual trafficking, sexual violence and coercion, and female genital cutting.

Recent international agreements, changes in countries' laws and policies, research efforts and a variety of programmes explicitly address discrimination against girls and women, challenging the underlying values that perpetuate gender inequality.

Early and Child Marriage

Despite a shift towards later marriages in many parts of the world (see below), 82 million girls in developing countries who are now aged 10 to 17 will be married before their 18th birthday.[6] In some countries, the majority of girls still marry before age 18. These include: 60 per cent in Nepal, 76 per cent in Niger and 50 per cent in India.[7]

Factors perpetuating early marriage include poverty, parental desire to ensure sexual relations within marriage, a lack of educational or employment opportunities for girls, the sense that girls' main value is as wives and mothers, and dowry systems. Girls who become pregnant may face extreme pressure from families and communities to marry.

---

7 **RIGHTS DENIED BY CHILD OR EARLY MARRIAGE**
Early marriage of girls undermines a number of rights guaranteed by the Convention on the Rights of the Child:

- The right to education (Article 28).

- The right to be protected from all forms of physical or mental violence, injury or abuse, including sexual abuse (Article 19) and from all forms of sexual exploitation (Article 34).

- The right to the enjoyment of the highest attainable standard of health (Article 24).

- The right to educational and vocational information and guidance (Article 28).

- The right to seek, receive and impart information and ideas (Article 13).

- The right to rest and leisure, and to participate freely in cultural life (Article 31).

- The right to not be separated from their parents against their will (Article 9).

- The right to protection against all forms of exploitation affecting any aspect of the child's welfare (Article 36).

The age at which people marry in a particular culture reflects the way family life is organized and the opportunities young men and women have as they assume adult responsibilities.[8]

Early marriage violates a number of girls' human rights (see Box 7) and vastly increases the risks to girls' and infants' health and opportunities.

AGE AT MARRIAGE RISING The proportion of marriages in which the woman is in her teens has declined considerably over the past 30 years.[9] The reduction has been largest in Africa: over 0.75 per cent per year. Declines in South and South-east Asia and in the Arab States have also been notable but smaller, over 0.5 per cent per year.

While earlier sexual debut and marriage are more common among less-educated women,[10] increases in educational enrolment explain only a small share of the documented increase in marriage age. Declines in arranged marriages, changes in marriage laws,[11] increases in urbanization and changing norms about the desirability of early marriage all contribute.

MEN MARRY LATER Differences between the age at marriage for men and women (as well as how the marriage is decided and the kind of union) can significantly affect the power balance between spouses and the closeness of their partnership. Men marry much later than women.[12] Only in Middle Africa and South Central Asia are more than 5 per cent of men 15-19 married.[13] In the developed countries, less than 1 per cent of men marry so young.[14] In contrast, more than a quarter of women 15-19 in sub-Saharan Africa and South Central Asia—and in some countries more than half[15] —are married.

In all subregions in the developing world, between 9 and 40 per cent of men have married by age 20-24, compared to between 24 and 75 per cent of women of the same age group.[16] Sixty-five per cent or more of women 20-24 years of age are married in several subregions in Africa and Asia.[17]

Age differences between spouses vary by region, with the smallest difference—under 3 years—observed in Latin America, most of Oceania and the more-developed regions. Differences above 6 years are found in sub-Saharan Africa. The younger the girl, the larger the age gap is likely to be, and in 16 sub-Saharan African countries husbands of girls 15-19 are on average at least 10 years older.[18] These age differences reflect expectations about male earning capacity, female fecundity and a balance of power that favours men over women.

For many girls, marriage (and their sexual experience) starts when they are young, to husbands who are much

---

8 **AFGHAN TEENS SPEAK OUT AGAINST EARLY MARRIAGE** After a forum in Afghanistan on World Population Day 2003, adolescent girls spoke in favour of delaying early marriage to continue their education. "If my parents tried to force me to marry, I would refuse," declared Zohal, 16, as her fellow students nodded in agreement. The Afghan teenagers had just heard government leaders say that early marriage closes girls' educational prospects and threatens their health. Such outspokenness is rare in a country where conservative traditions hold firm, daughters bring a dowry and early pregnancy contributes to soaring rates of maternal mortality.

Zohal wants to go to university and study economics. She wishes all Afghan girls could attend school. "Our country has many problems after 20 years of war," Zohal added. "We need good doctors to help our people. We need schools; in many villages, there are no schools. People have to be literate to develop Afghanistan. Girls have to finish their studies; they have human rights." The Afghan Deputy Minister of Health, Deputy Minister of Women's Affairs, General Director of the Literacy Department and UNFPA Chief of Operations in Afghanistan all emphasized the importance of educating girls, protecting their health and delaying marriage and childbirth.

---

older and chosen for them by their parents, sometimes to men they have not met prior to their wedding day.

EDUCATION INTERRUPTED Young women in the developing world who marry in their early teens are denied much of what young people elsewhere take for granted: education, good health and access to care, economic opportunities and the right to associate with their peers, to name a few. Early marriage almost inevitably disrupts education, reducing opportunities for future independence through work.

Married girls are rarely found in school (often due to laws or school practices), and girls who are not in school rarely have much contact with their peers or people outside their families.[19]

Research from Bangladesh shows that expectations that husbands should be better educated than wives causes parents worried about over-educating their daughters to pull them out of school.[20] However, increased school enrolment contributes to later marriage: in India and Pakistan, for example, girls' staying in school longer has contributed directly to a decline in marriage before age 14.[21]

The consequences of early marriage for adolescent girls' sexual and reproductive health and rights are significant (see Chapter 4). Their exposure to STIs and HIV rises. Married girls are generally unable to negotiate condom use or to refuse sexual relations, and are more likely to be married to older men with more sexual experience who are more likely than single men to be HIV-positive.[22] Indeed, recent research in Kenya and Zambia suggests that married girls are more likely to be HIV positive than their unmarried counterparts.[23]

Young married women often cannot seek health care without the permission of their husbands or other family members, generally cannot pay for health care independently and may experience periods of depression. Husbands and families also apply considerable pressure on young wives to have a child soon after marriage, increasing their risk of maternal death or injury and hampering efforts to prevent STIs and HIV through regular condom use. Early childbearing often goes hand in hand with high rates of poverty, lower levels of education, less mobility and fewer attended births.[24]

In addition, adolescent girls' relative lack of power is often linked to violence in marriage, which is associated with unwanted pregnancy and STIs.[25] Child or adolescent brides have very little ability to leave abusive partners, and many live in isolation with little chance to secure social or legal support to remedy their situation.

DELAYING EARLY MARRIAGE In most places, persistent early childbearing is a public health concern. Efforts to delay marriage and increase age at the first birth include enforcement of existing laws, expansion of schooling and provision of job training.

The Government of Nepal, in collaboration with UNFPA, has educated adults about the harm that very early marriage can cause, and has created materials encouraging parents to delay marrying their daughters

before age 20.[26] The Chinese Government has made efforts to reduce very early marriages arranged by parents.[27]

One district in Rajasthan, in northern India, has conducted a public education campaign encouraging families to prolong engagements—often entered into when girls are age 7 or 8—before the marriage is consummated and brides move to the grooms' homes.[28] In southern India, the NGO Myrada has organized children's groups in one community to address child marriage and bonded labour.[29] Working with parents and other adults, the children were able to convince some businesspeople to free children from servitude and parents to delay the marriages of their young daughters.

Providing opportunities for girls to continue their education or earn money is another strategy for delaying marriage as well as expanding life skills and choices. The garment industry in Bangladesh has extended the period before marriage by providing young women with the means to earn a living.[30] Also in Bangladesh, a secondary school scholarship programme for girls, requiring a commitment that girls remain unmarried through the tenth standard final examination, was so successful that the Government has expanded it to the national level.[31] There was an immediate effect in delaying marriage.[32] In areas targeted by the project, female enrolment more than doubled between 1994 and 2001.[33]

Several Indian states have also developed long-term investment programmes that offer young women money or gifts when they have completed a certain level of schooling and are still unmarried.[34] And countries in Eastern Europe and the Baltic States experienced rapid declines in adolescent fertility in the 1990s as a result of increasing school enrolment.[35]

Changing Norms, Difficult Challenges

In several regions of the world, the age of marriage is increasing, the age of sexual maturity is decreasing[36] and "sexual debut" is occurring earlier in young people's lives, lengthening the time when women and men face risks to their health.

In most settings, gender norms shape young women's and men's early sexual experiences. Young women are often pressured or coerced to accept risky sexual behaviour, while young men are encouraged to take sexual risks—and may well expect their partners to comply or face intimidation or violence. Early sexual experience is often associated with other risky behaviours like alcohol and drug use or smoking, particularly for boys.

Many girls' first sexual experiences involve coercion.[37] The younger the girl and the greater the age difference

| 9 | **ENSURING MARRIED ADOLESCENTS' REPRODUCTIVE HEALTH** In Bangladesh, Pathfinder has developed a Newlywed Programme to support young couples in planning their childbearing, in delaying the first birth, spacing their children, and in seeking prenatal care. An assessment found that female newlyweds rarely leave the home, and they report that life is worse since marriage because they have so little freedom. Young married men, in contrast, have a much wider social range, and spend much of their free time outside the household.

Young couples have many concerns about sexuality. They identified programme staff as having an important influence on their decision-making. Further work needs to be done to reduce the barriers young women face in seeking out health services and information outside their marital households.

between her and the male, the greater the likelihood of an exploitive relationship.

Unequal gender norms persist in many parts of the world, with young men often encouraged to enlarge their sexual experiences while restraint is urged on young women. In some settings, the balance may be highly skewed, with very high demands for women to remain chaste coupled with few demands (if any) on men to practise sexual self-control or to treat partners with respect. For young men and women, these different expectations are harmful and have a negative impact on the establishment of healthy, responsible and equitable relationships.

Studies in 21 countries indicate that more than one third of boys' first sexual experience is with a sex worker. Sexually active boys report having sexual relations with a variety of partners, including girlfriends, informal female acquaintances and sex workers.[38]

Young women generally engage in sexual relations within the context of a relationship, and see it as a means of strengthening the relationship. Low power, fear of violence, and a sense of "marital duty" prevent many women from discussing the timing of their sexual relations with their husbands.

Unequal gender norms, including expectations of female passivity, often reduce young women's ability to make informed choices about their sexual health. Fear of losing one's partner can also limit their choices. Studies in the United States suggest that among girls abandoned after sexual initiation, the resulting depression is as intense as that which follows the death of a family member.[39]

Male sexual behaviour reflects and affirms masculine identity in all cultures. But cultural concepts of identity vary. Changing social and cultural conditions (e.g., more education, the changing nature of work, access to mass media, women's empowerment, generational value shifts, increases in informal unions, decreased roles for extended family, increased costs of child-raising, urbanization and international migration) are redefining accepted concepts of masculinity and male-female relationships, with an increased focus on responsibility.

DATING AND RELATIONSHIPS Patterns of relationships between young men and young women are changing.[40] Rising age at marriage increases the opportunity for friendships, dating and more serious partnerships between young males and females. Its prevalence varies in different settings and social contexts.

In some settings, dating is common, if irregular, among large proportions of youth, but the relationship contents vary. The intensity of relationships varies with age: college students more commonly form close attachments. For the great majority of youth (particularly in Eastern and Western Asia) these do not include sexual relations.

Parental oversight of adolescent relationships is common, but large minorities—larger for males than females—form attachments without permission. Recent research in the United States[41] indicates that at least a fifth of young adolescents are engaging in sexual relationships, often without parental knowledge. Adult knowledge of their children's sexual experience is often limited.

In settings where values insist on premarital abstinence, there is a greater tendency to withhold information about sexual and reproductive health from youth and from policy discussion.

EARLIER ONSET OF SEXUAL ACTIVITY Sexual initiation is increasingly occurring outside of marriage, particularly

---

IO **GENDERED BEHAVIOUR** Focus group research in South Africa found that gender norms limit young women's negotiating power to protect themselves in sexual encounters. "Dominant social norms of masculinity portrayed young men as conquering heroes and macho risk-takers in the sexual arena," while young women were predisposed "to use the responses of passivity or fruitless resistance in the face of male advances".

Girls tend to say the reason they engage in sexual activity is to cement a relationship with someone they love. If they insist on condom use, it may jeopardize that relationship. Young men may capitalize on this emotion when seeking to engage in sex with young women.

In Senegal, young people aged 14-16 in focus groups agreed that a lack of respect characterizes expectations of relationships. Boys suspected girls of being primarily interested in money and other material things, while both stated that girls who refuse to have sex face the possibility of beatings or rape.

Rio de Janeiro's *Instituto Promundo*

researched what makes some young men behave more positively towards women than others. The "gender-equitable" men sought relationships based on equality and intimacy rather than sexual conquest, opposed violence against women, wanted to share responsibility in caring for their children and wanted to have some responsibility for reproductive health. This research gave rise to a programme promoting a healthy masculinity among adolescent boys through activities to raise awareness around violence against women and promote good health.

for boys. Both adolescent boys and girls who engage in sexual activity often begin with little knowledge of sexuality, reproductive health, safer sexual practices, or their right to refuse and to abstain.

In Peru, the Philippines, Thailand and Viet Nam, both young men and young women are more likely to consider premarital sex to be more acceptable for males than for females.[42] Young men tend to begin having sex at least two to three years before young women—in some parts of the world within the context of sexual initiation rites or with a sex worker.[43]

In Brazil, Ethiopia, Gabon, Haiti, Kenya, Latvia, Malawi, Nicaragua and Poland, more than one quarter of young men aged 15-19 interviewed said they first had sex before age 15.[44] In Latin America and the Caribbean, the average age at first sexual encounter is earlier for males than females, ranging from 12.7 years for boys and 15.6 for girls in Jamaica to 16.0 for boys and 17.9 for girls in Chile.[45]

One in-depth study uncovered two patterns of young men's first sexual experiences—findings that parallel other research.[46] The first pattern, termed "impulsive", took place at an early age (15 or younger), motivated by curiosity, reported "physical need" or peer pressure. It usually occurred in a hotel or brothel with a sex worker. Condoms were used, if any contraception was. In the second pattern, "occasional", young men's first sexual experience took place with a friend or casual acquaintance in varied locations, often spontaneously and without contraception.

Premarital sexual activity for adolescent girls varies considerably in different regions: less than 12 per cent in Asia, up to a quarter in Latin America and around half in sub-Saharan Africa.

In sub-Saharan Africa in particular, girls' early sexual relationships are very likely to occur with men who are considerably older, often in exchange for money or gifts. These conditions significantly reduce girls' ability to negotiate safer sex and increase their chances of contracting STIs and HIV or becoming pregnant. Because cross-generational sex is driven in part by poverty, and is also seen as a way to increase one's status, parents sometimes encourage it.[47]

As couples move towards marriage, premarital sex may well occur in a majority of relationships, even in relatively conservative settings.[48]

A lack of other opportunities such as employment, sports, or religious and cultural activities tends to increase the centrality of sexual behaviour in adolescents' self-definition and self-esteem.

UNWANTED PREGNANCY Many young men and women are beginning sexual activity earlier in life. By not choosing abstinence as an option, a larger proportion of adolescents and young people need access to family planning methods to avoid unwanted pregnancies.[49]

Due to limited knowledge and guidance, adolescents are less likely to practise safer sex or to use contraception. Contraceptive use is still infrequent in most early sexual experiences. Young women consistently report lower usage rates than men, evidence of their unequal power in negotiating use of family planning with their partner or restrictions on their access to services (due to lack of information, shame, laws, health provider attitudes and practices or social mores).

Community studies suggest that between 10 and 40 per cent of young, unmarried women have experienced unwanted pregnancy. At the high end, in studies of soon-to-be married women, unmarried factory workers, out-of-school adolescents and women seeking health care, more than one third had an unwanted pregnancy.[50]

A majority of unwanted pregnancies among young, unmarried women end in abortion,[51] posing a serious public health concern since many—if not most—of these abortions are unsafe, carried out by people lacking formal medical training and in facilities with substandard hygiene and care.

Studies in four Latin American countries found that between 10 and 14 per cent of pregnancies among young, never-married women ended in abortion; four other countries show levels half as high. The pattern in Asia is diverse in the few countries where studies have been undertaken.[52] In Kazakhstan, where recourse to abortion for unwanted pregnancy has been accepted historically, rates remain high, about 45 per cent; by contrast, in the Philippines, it is relatively rare (about 7 per cent) and births after marriage predominate.[53]

CONTRACEPTIVE USE Detailed data on premarital sexual behaviour have only recently been collected in developing countries. In 13 countries with appropriate surveys of the timing of different sexual and reproductive behaviours, large differentials are observed in the age of sexual debut and in the proportion of sexual activity protected by contraception.[54]

Women from the three Asian countries studied[55] were highly likely to remain virgins until marriage (above 95 per cent in two of the countries), but once sexually active they were less likely to be protected by contraceptive use. Premarital virginity rates in Latin America[56] varied from 58 per cent (Colombia) to 90 per cent (Nicaragua), and in Africa from 45 per cent (Kenya) to 73 per cent (Zimbabwe).

In the Latin American and African countries studied, more than 40 per cent of pregnancies to sexually active unmarried women resulted in live births prior to marriage. Live births shortly after marriage were common in all regions. In only two Latin American countries (Brazil and Colombia) was more than half of the sexual activity between sexual initiation and marriage protected by contraception. Most commonly, two thirds to three quarters of sexual activity was unprotected.

As young couples establish long-term relationships, they are more likely to practise contraception, but tend to use methods other than condoms—hampering their ability to protect themselves from sexually transmitted infections, including HIV.[57]

Parental and Family Support

Caring, supportive and trusted adults are essential to the healthy development of adolescents and young people. Building a relationship of trust and open communication, early on, contributes to greater confidence and self-esteem, which helps young people to avoid risky behaviour. Efforts to encourage parent and child communication are very important. Orphaned children, or those who have run away from home or are struggling to survive on their own, also need trusted adults to guide them.

Innovative HIV/AIDS prevention and reproductive health programmes are working with parents to foster better communication about sexuality and reproductive health. In one UNFPA-supported programme in Cambodia, parents and families were provided with brown paper bags filled with reproductive health information. Health and outreach workers then visited families to discuss the materials, listen to concerns, answer questions and provide health service referrals, if needed.

Successful programmes encourage parents to engage their daughters and sons in discussions on the larger issues of relationships, goals and aspirations. In South Africa, the national youth HIV-prevention programme, loveLife, believes that open, early and frank discussion of sexuality is key to reducing HIV infection in the country. The programme encourages parents to tell their children to delay sexual activity; to talk about the pressures to engage in sexual activity; to talk about the values of love, respect, dignity, and responsibility that should shape attitudes to relationships; to talk about protection and safety when sexually active; and to use available sources of information.

Reaching out to parents and families helps build community support for adolescent sexual and reproductive health, which remains a sensitive issue in most societies.

Sexual Violence and Trafficking

Sexual violence is common in the lives of adolescent girls. This gross violation of their rights also harms their reproductive and sexual health. Only over the past decade has the extent of sexual violence against girls come to be understood and documentation begun. Studies in India, Jamaica, Mali, the United Republic of Tanzania and Zimbabwe found that between 20 and 30 per cent of adolescent girls had experienced sexual violence.[58]

COERCION The first sexual experience for many adolescent girls is forced. In South Africa, 30 per cent of young women indicate that their first sex was coerced. Sexual violence undermines girls' development by making it difficult for them to remain in school, destroying their confidence in adults and in peers, and putting them at risk of STIs, unwanted pregnancy and short- and long-term physical or psychological damage.

Male adolescents and adult men often tolerate or even condone sexual coercion. Young women, too, may view sexual violence or sex that is obtained through force, fear or intimidation as normal, reflecting perverse gender norms in some communities or societies.

One study in South Africa found that sexual violence and coercion against young girls was so widespread it was referred to as "everyday love."[59] In another study of 30,000 young people, one man in four claimed to have had sex without a girl's consent.[60] Most young men and women expressed the belief that forcing oneself on someone one knows is simply "rough sex", and not sexual violence, and the majority of women stated that women were responsible for sexual abuse.

The circumstances of sexual violence almost everywhere are similar: girls are most often raped or otherwise abused by people they know, including family members. Sometimes assailants are respected members of their communities: teachers, employers and even religious leaders. Educators increasingly recognize the need to be proactive in countering the violence. The School of Public Health at the University of the Western Cape in South Africa developed an approach to combating sexual and gender-based violence as early as primary school, challenging teachers' attitudes and encouraging them to convey anti-violence messages to students.

TRAFFICKING IN YOUNG WOMEN AND GIRLS Estimates of the number of women and children trafficked each year into the sex trade (often through coercion or abduction) and labour enslavement vary widely, ranging between 700,000 and 4 million.[61] The selling of young women into sexual bondage, a serious violation of their rights and threat to their health, has grown considerably over the past decade.[62] Extreme poverty, the low status of women and girls, lax border checks, and the collusion of law enforcement all contribute to the expansion.

In Asia and Eastern Europe, girls as young as 13 are trafficked as "mail order brides".[63] In India, an estimated two in five sex workers are below age 18.[64] In Sri Lanka, a majority of child sex workers are boys.[65] According to one regional estimation, between 1-2 million men and women are trafficked annually, the majority in Asia. Over 225,000 originate in South East Asia, and an additional 150,000 in South Asia.[66]

Many women from the states of the former Soviet Union are taken to Israel, other parts of the Middle East or Western Europe; many are under age 16. The justice system in many countries is more likely to jail or expel the young women than to punish the traffickers.

Young sex workers are often kept from the view of authorities. In Cambodia, for example, an assessment of the 100 per cent condom use policy for sex workers found that young female sex workers were often hidden when police came to record their identities.[67]

Young sex workers, both female and male, are at high risk of HIV infection. They have little or no negotiating power to insist on condom use and are often targets of coerced or forced sex, which can increase the chances of HIV transmission. HIV prevalence among young sex workers tends to be high—from an estimated 25 per cent in Cambodia to 48 per cent in parts of India and 70 per cent in Abidjan, Côte d'Ivoire.[68]

Some countries have begun to challenge the trafficking trade, often in alliance with community leaders. Thailand's Government, for example, made assisting youth at risk of entering the sex industry a high priority in the early 1990s. Target areas include eight provinces in northern Thailand with high rates of HIV/AIDS and high percentages of girls who drop out of school.[69] Teachers are trained to identify girls at high risk of being sold, and to work with their families to keep them in school and to earn money locally.

Female Genital Cutting

Female genital cutting (FGC, also known as female genital mutilation or female circumcision) threatens the sexual and reproductive health of millions of girls in sub-Saharan Africa and the Middle East.

In the Sudan, infertility resulting from infibulation may be associated with higher rates of divorce.[70] Men's attitudes, particularly about controlling female sexuality, are an important factor in the perpetuation of FGC.[71]

Worldwide, about 130 million girls and young women have experienced FGC and an additional 2 million are at risk each year (6,000 every day). FGC is practised in about 28 countries, with prevalence rates ranging from 5 per cent in the Democratic Republic of Congo to 98 per cent in Somalia, the Arabian Peninsula and the Gulf Region.[72] Studies done in 1995 found 97 per cent of married women in Egypt aged 15 to 49 had been circumcised; in Mali, this figure in 1998 was 94 per cent.[73]

Most procedures are done by non-medical personnel—including traditional birth attendants, midwives, and "old women"—using unsterilized blades or string, increasing chances of infection; usually post-operative or emergency treatment is not readily available.[74]

WAYS OF REDUCING FGC Many countries have passed laws banning FGC, including Burkina Faso, Djibouti, Egypt, Ghana, Senegal, Togo and the United Republic of Tanzania. While these laws call for fines and jail terms,[75] enforcement is often lax and the practice continues, cloaked in greater secrecy.

Efforts are under way to reduce the incidence of FGC and to change underlying attitudes about female sexuality and worth. In Kenya, the United Nations Development Fund for Women (UNIFEM), the NGO *Maendeleo ya Wanawake* Organization (MYWO) and the Program for Appropriate Technology in Health have promoted "Circumcision through Words", an alternative rite of passage that preserves positive aspects of the cultural tradition.[76] Kenya's Children Act, passed in 2001, prohibits FGC.[77] A week-long programme of seclusion, traditional teachings, health education and counselling is followed by a community-wide celebration with food, dancing and singing, all affirming the joyous transition to womanhood.

In addition to community leaders, the project has involved men and boys, especially fathers and brothers; boys have refused to marry girls who have undergone FGC, reassuring parents about the future marriageability of uncircumcised daughters. In January 2000, UNFPA and several other UN agencies signed an agreement to extend this effort to other communities with high rates of FGC.

In Senegal, the organization Tostan has worked to raise awareness of health and rights, resulting in group decisions in 938 villages (18 per cent of 5,000 registered communities) to abandon FGC and early marriage.[78] In Mali, Healthy Tomorrow takes a more explicitly critical approach, using music to educate people about the harm done by the practice.[79]

3 hiv/aids and adolescents

HIV/AIDS has become a disease of young people, with young adults aged 15-24 accounting for half of the some 5 million new cases of HIV infection worldwide each year. Yet young people often lack the information, skills and services they need to protect themselves from HIV infection. Providing these is crucial to turning back the epidemic.

An estimated 6,000 youth a day become infected with HIV/AIDS—one every 14 seconds—the majority of them young women. At the end of 2001, an estimated 11.8 million young people aged 15-24 were living with HIV/AIDS, one third of the global total of people living with HIV/AIDS. Only a small percentage of these young people know they are HIV-positive.[1] (See Table 4).

In addition, more than 13 million children under age 15 have lost one or both parents to AIDS. The overwhelming majority of these AIDS orphans live in Africa. By 2010, their number is projected to reach 25 million.[3]

Contributing Factors

A combination of social, biological and economic factors help fuel the AIDS pandemic:

POVERTY HIV/AIDS is a disease highly associated with poverty. A World Bank study of 72 countries showed that both low per capita income and high-income inequality were linked to high national HIV infection rates, and a $2,000 increase in per capita income was associated with a 4 per cent reduction in infections.[4] The 2001 United Nations General Assembly Special Session on HIV/AIDS recognized that "poverty, underdevelopment and illiteracy are among the principal contributing factors to the spread of HIV/AIDS".

GIRLS AND WOMEN ARE MORE VULNERABLE For reasons of biology, gender and cultural norms, females are more susceptible than males to HIV infection. Thus an estimated 7.3 million young women are living with HIV/AIDS compared to 4.5 million young men. Two thirds of newly infected youth aged 15-19 in sub-Saharan Africa are female. Among women, the peak age for HIV prevalence tends to be around age 25, 10 to 15 years younger than the peak age for men.[5]

Biologically, the risk of infection during unprotected sex is two to four times higher for women than men;[6] young women are even more vulnerable because their reproductive tracts are still maturing and tears in the tissue allow easy access to infection.[7]

Socially, young women also face higher risks. When they have sexual relations, it tends to be with older men, increasing the likelihood that their partners are already infected. Some adolescent girls are attached to "sugar daddies", much older, relatively well-off (usually married) men who support them in exchange for sex. More commonly, sexually active adolescent girls, in Africa at least, have partners 2-10 years their senior who provide them with gifts, such as soap, perfume, meals out and jewellery.

Table 4: Young People 15-24 Living with HIV/AIDS, by Sex, December 2001[2]

Region	Young Women per cent	Young Men per cent	Total
Sub-Saharan Africa	67	33	8,600,000
North Africa and the Middle East	41	59	160,000
East Asia and the Pacific	49	51	740,000
South Asia	62	38	1,100,000
Central Asia and Eastern Europe	35	65	430,000
Latin America and the Caribbean	31	69	560,000
Industrialized countries	33	67	240,000
World	62	38	11,800,000

Source: UNICEF/UNAIDS/WHO.

Figure 4: New HIV Infections in 2002, by Age Group

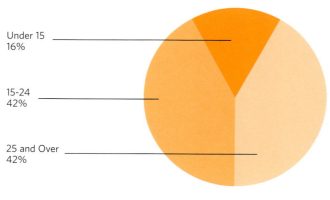

Under 15
16%

15-24
42%

25 and Over
42%

Source: UNAIDS

Some poor girls exchange sex for money for school fees or to help their families. Once in these relationships with teachers, drivers, shopkeepers or even policemen, girls have little power to negotiate the use of condoms.[8]

Men often seek younger sexual partners who are unlikely to be infected with HIV.[9]

The common myth in some places that sex with a virgin can cure AIDS or STIs further endangers young girls who fall prey to forced or coerced sexual relations.

MARRIED YOUTH AT RISK Marriage does not always protect young women against HIV infection. Since a much higher percentage of young men than young women become sexually active early, young women are likely to marry an already sexually experienced man. In Pune, India, a study in an STI clinic found that 25 per cent of the 4,000 women attending the clinic were infected with an STI and 14 per cent were HIV positive. Among the 93 per cent who were married, 91 per cent had only one partner, their husbands.

A study in Kisumu, Kenya, found that as many as half of the married women whose husbands were 10 or more years older were infected with HIV, compared to none of the women whose husbands were only up to three years older.[10]

Within marriage it is particularly difficult for women to negotiate condom use, especially if they are much younger than their husbands.

LACK OF INFORMATION AND SKILLS FOR PROTECTION
Because sex is a taboo topic in many countries, large numbers of young people do not get sufficient information—or the skills—to refuse sex or negotiate safer sex practices. While most young people have heard about HIV/AIDS, few know enough to protect themselves against infection.

Surveys from 40 countries indicate that more than half of the young people have misconceptions about how HIV is transmitted.[11] In Ukraine, while 100 per cent of adolescent females know about AIDS, only 21 per cent know of three methods of prevention. In Somalia, only 26 per cent of adolescent females have heard of AIDS and only 1 per cent know how to protect themselves. In Botswana, where one in three people is living with HIV/AIDS, virtually all young people have heard of AIDS and more than 75 per cent know the three primary means of protection. Still, 62 per cent of girls had at least one major misconception about how HIV is spread. Far too many young people think they can tell if someone is HIV positive simply by looking at them.

FEELINGS OF INVINCIBILITY Adolescents tend to underestimate, downplay or deny their risks of HIV infection. Case studies by the World Health Organization (WHO) indicate that only between one fifth and one third consider themselves at risk.[12] Many young people do not recognize that their partner's behaviour also puts them at risk. Still others may perceive HIV as something that occurs only among sex workers, drug users or men who share intimate relations. Feelings of invincibility, combined with the lack of awareness of the consequences of risky behaviour, may make them less likely to take precautions to protect their health—and lives.

SEXUALLY TRANSMITTED INFECTIONS Sexually transmitted infections increase the likelihood of HIV transmission considerably,[13] as well as having other reproductive health consequences such as chronic pain, infertility or life-threatening ectopic pregnancies. While data on STIs in developing countries are scarce, particularly for young people, WHO estimates that at least a third of the more than 333 million new cases of curable STIs each year occur among people under age 25.[14] Young people are also substantially more likely than adults to become re-infected after having been treated.

A study in South Africa showed that adolescent girls were 30 per cent more likely to get STIs than were boys, in large part because they were involved with older males who were more likely to have STIs themselves.[15]

Studies on gonorrhoea in selected Middle Eastern and African countries found infection levels were highest among the 15-19 age group.[16] A substantial minority of young people, more men than women, have experienced symptoms of STIs, according to studies from Argentina, Botswana, Peru, the Philippines, the Republic of Korea and Thailand.[17]

Knowledge about STIs is generally poor among young people. A study among young sex workers in Cambodia found that their limited knowledge was based on a mixture of facts, myths and rumours and was not always correct.[18] An unfortunate misconception among many young people, including in Kampala, Uganda, and Ho Chi Minh City, Viet Nam, is that STI symptoms will go away over time or that good personal hygiene will prevent STIs (and HIV). One in five female university students in Ilorin, Nigeria, 30 per cent of youth in parts of Chile and half of young men and women in sites in Guatemala also hold this belief.[19]

Young people are more likely to seek traditional remedies for STIs, or to ignore the symptoms. This pattern is attributed to feelings of guilt over having an STI and to the stigmatizing treatment they tend to receive in health care centres, including STI clinics.

ALCOHOL AND DRUG USE Sharing needles for drug use is a highly efficient means of spreading HIV because the virus is injected directly into the blood stream. Mixing drug use with sex for money provides a bridge for HIV from injecting drug users to the wider community.

Drug use often starts in adolescence. In Nepal, where half of the country's 50,000 injecting drug users are 16 to 25 years old, the incidence of HIV among people who inject drugs climbed from 2 per cent in 1995 to nearly 50 per cent in 1998.[20] The Russian Federation's HIV epidemic is the fastest growing in the world, fuelled by the rising number of young drug users. In China, HIV rates are highest among injecting drug users, typically young men.

The number of drug addicts is rising, particularly in Eastern and Central Europe, as is the number of occasional users. According to 2000 figures from UNAIDS, injecting drug use accounts for more than half of all HIV cases in Argentina, Bahrain, China, Georgia, Iran, Italy, Kazakhstan, Latvia, Moldova, Portugal, the Russian Federation, Spain and Ukraine.[21]

Alcohol use can also fuel the HIV epidemic by increasing risky sexual behaviour. A study in Rwanda found that young people aged 15-24 who consumed alcohol were less likely to abstain from sex.[22] In a study of young adolescents in Jamaica, those who had experimented with alcohol were 2.4 times more likely than others to say they had sexual activity, other factors being equal.[23]

INTERACTION WITH TUBERCULOSIS Tuberculosis is the leading cause of death among AIDS patients worldwide. One third of all AIDS patients are infected with tuberculosis. Those infected with HIV are much more likely than others—800 times, by some estimates—of developing active tuberculosis.[24] In Kenya, the prevalence of both HIV and tuberculosis doubled between 1990 and 1996.[25]

Young people should receive vaccinations to prevent tuberculosis.[26] Most tuberculosis is treatable using directly observed therapy. Leaving it half-treated or mistreated can result in drug-resistant tuberculosis, which is harder and much more expensive to treat. Thus, tuberculosis control programmes, including for young people, must be an integral part of AIDS prevention and care strategies.

Regional Differences

By far, the fastest spread of HIV/AIDS among young people is in sub-Saharan Africa, where an estimated 8.6 million youth (67 per cent of them female) are living with HIV/AIDS. In Botswana, South Africa and Zimbabwe, an estimated 60 per cent of boys now 15 years old will eventually become infected.[27]

HIV is also spreading rapidly in South Asia, where an estimated 1.1 million youth are infected (62 per cent female). In parts of South India, the epidemic has crossed over from sex workers and injecting drug users to the general population.

In Latin America and the Caribbean, an estimated 560,000 youth are living with HIV/AIDS (31 per cent female). A few Caribbean countries have some of the most serious epidemics outside Africa, with at least 2 per cent of young women infected. In Latin America the virus has spread mainly among men who are sexually active with other men, but it is moving beyond that population to young women.

East and South-east Asia have an estimated 740,000 youth living with HIV/AIDS, roughly half of whom are female. Given China's large population and rising incidence of HIV, the number of youth with HIV/AIDS in this region is likely to grow considerably. Epidemics once concentrated among injecting drug users and commercial sex workers have now spread to the general population in Cambodia, Myanmar and Thailand. (Though Thailand has effectively reduced prevalence.)

Infection rates are rising rapidly in Eastern and Central Europe. In 2001, an estimated 430,000 youth were living with HIV/AIDS (35 per cent female). The epidemic is growing in this region due mainly to intravenous drug use, particularly among young men, but also to trafficking of women and sex work.

There were an estimated 160,000 infected youth (41 per cent female) in the Middle East and North Africa in 2001. Although surveillance systems in this region have improved in the past few years, this estimate may be low. While there is little sexual contact among unmarried young people, the region needs to be vigilant and raise awareness. There is evidence of rising STI rates—a precursor for increasing HIV infections. High rates of injecting drug use in some areas also indicate the likely spread of HIV.

In North America and Western Europe, the epidemic is fairly contained, except among the poor and minorities, drug users and sex workers, particularly young women. Still, complacency, particularly among young people, may be undoing the gains made in slowing the spread of HIV.

Impact of AIDS on Young People

ADOLESCENT ORPHANS Youth who have lost one or both parents to AIDS (see Chapter 1) are particularly vulnerable to infection themselves. Many face exploitation, including physical and sexual abuse. With weakened family support, some engage in risky sexual behaviour or inject drugs. Those forced to live on the streets may turn to sex work and crime as a means to survive.[28] After suffering the emotional toll of losing their parents, many also face stigma and discrimination.

EDUCATION Young people infected or affected by HIV/AIDS frequently have their schooling disrupted.[29] Dropping out is common, particularly for girls who have to care for sick family members or their siblings to keep the family together. Inability to pay school fees also forces boys and girls to leave school. Others drop out because of stigma and discrimination by schools, teachers or classmates.

Teachers are also succumbing to HIV/AIDS. UNAIDS estimates that in 2001 as many as 1 million children and young people in sub-Saharan Africa lost their teachers to AIDS.[30]

Growing up without an education has lifetime effects. Survey data from countries around the world show that when parents are not alive, children ages 10-14 are less likely to be in school than are children of the same age whose parents are alive. In Madagascar, for example, the percentages of orphaned children ages 10-14 in school is 34 per cent compared to 65 per cent of non-orphaned children. In Indonesia, the percentages are 65 and 85, respectively.[31]

Social Marketing of Contraceptives

The "ABC" approach, Abstinence, Be faithful, and use Condoms (as detailed in Chapter 4) has proven effective. Social marketing combines market research and advertising techniques with health promotion through mass media, peer promoters and community-based events. Condoms are usually the product that is marketed, often with a "dual protection" message to help protect against both pregnancy and STIs including HIV. Nearly any place where young people spend time and congregate, from school to work to discos, is a potential site for information provision and condom availability.

Social marketing, like mass media, can be targeted to specific groups. In Indonesia, a successful campaign to increase condom use among commercial sex workers combined print media, events at bars and universities, counselling on condom negotiation and education of brothel owners. As a result, the percentage of sex workers using condoms increased from 36 to 48.[32]

The Social Marketing for Adolescent Sexual Health (SMASH) programme, carried out by Population Services International, evaluated activities in urban areas of Botswana, Cameroon, Guinea and South Africa. Initiatives used schools, mass media, youth clubs and peer interventions to raise awareness and promote safer sex practices, especially condom use, among young people.

While these activities succeeded in raising awareness of the benefits of protective behaviour including abstinence and condom use, and in reducing the barriers to condom use, they were less successful in changing behaviour. It had more success among young women than among young men, suggesting that the two groups need to be reached in different ways.[33]

Building on lessons learned from the SMASH programme in Cameroon, another social marketing programme was initiated there in 2000. The first phase used a mass-media campaign, radio call-in shows, a newspaper, peer educators and a radio drama to promote consistent condom use, particularly with regular partners. Activities in the current phase encourage parents to talk to their children about HIV/AIDS prevention, empower girls to negotiate abstinence or condom use, and emphasize the importance of using condoms consistently with regular partners.[34]

II | **THE ABC APPROACH** In 2001, the United Nations General Assembly Special Session (UNGASS) endorsed the ABC approach to preventing HIV infection. The ABC approach to behaviour change gives three clear messages for preventing the transmission of HIV. ABC stands for: Abstain from having sexual relations or, for youth, delay having sex; Be faithful to one uninfected partner; and use Condoms consistently and correctly.

Sometimes D, for Drugs, is added to the message, referring to intravenous drug use and recreational use of alcohol, which can increase the likelihood of unsafe sex. Some also refer to ABC+, which includes the message to get tested and treated for STIs (which increase the risk of transmission of HIV in unprotected sex). Each component of the ABC message should be presented in a comprehensive and balanced way. (See Chapter 4.)

There are many negative and often mistaken attitudes about condom use. Some young people do not believe the condom offers reliable protection against unwanted pregnancy or even HIV. In a study in Kenya, only 35 per cent of urban students and 56 per cent of rural students expressed confidence in the effectiveness of condoms.[35] A study in Botswana found that 76 per cent of boys were convinced that condoms often slide off.[36] Another study in Botswana indicated that some youth believe condoms spread infection.[37] Negative perceptions about the condom were also found to be a major obstacle in prevention activities in Suriname.[38]

Young men in a focus group discussion in South Africa said they did not have the courage to ask for condoms in pharmacies and clinics. They said pharmacy or clinic staff expressed displeasure at the sexual activity of young people. The young men said they would like to be able to get condoms in game arcades, public toilets, nightclubs, music shops, internet cafes and vending machines—and from their peers rather than from adults. Some also expressed discomfort using condoms due to inexperience, and seemed more worried about maintaining their image than about the risks of unprotected sex.[39]

Despite these drawbacks, an evaluation concluded that, "Social marketing approaches directed at youth appear to hold significant promise for promoting condom use on a relatively large scale and for making regular condom use socially acceptable. Media efforts should be combined with pharmacies and other private-sector outlets that young people prefer for reasons of confidentiality and convenience, and should be combined with training to make these services more youth friendly."[40]

Services for HIV/AIDS Prevention and Care

Voluntary counselling and testing (VCT) services are a vital part of HIV prevention, treatment and care programmes. Regardless of the result, young people tested often change to less risky behaviour. Studies show that many young people need and want access to VCT so they can learn whether they are infected—provided the services are confidential and affordable and that they are given the results honestly.[41]

However, a barrier to testing is the lack of treatment and support for those who test positive. Few young people in the developing world have access to antiretroviral drugs (ARVs) to treat HIV. In fact, of the people in the developing world who would benefit from ARVs, fewer than 5 per cent currently get them.[42] Botswana and Brazil have pledged to provide ARVs to all who need them, but other hard-hit countries lack the resources to follow suit.

---

12 REACHING YOUTH THROUGH SOCIAL MARKETING
The SMASH assessment of condom social marketing activities aimed at young people in four African countries found that:

- Changing adolescent behaviour may require intensive efforts lasting at least two to three years.
- Programmes are most effective if they include a carefully designed mix of mass media promotion and face-to-face communication.
- Young men and women have different sexual health concerns that need to be addressed differently.
- Careful communication strategies are needed to reduce the stigma associated with condom use.
- Youth should be involved in programme design.

---

13 IMPROVING VOLUNTARY COUNSELLING AND TESTING FOR YOUTH Research and experience have identified qualities of effective, youth-friendly VCT programmes:

- Service providers trained to counsel youth about HIV.
- Use of a separate room or alternate site so youth will not encounter family members or adults they know when seeking VCT.
- Free or reduced price of tests for young people.
- Referral system for young clients.
- Outreach to schools and youth groups.
- Multimedia campaigns to inform youth about VCT.

As countries expand access to HIV treatment, use of VCT services should increase.

Even where treatment is not available, VCT can lead young people to change their behaviour. In a study in Kenya and Uganda, VCT was offered to young people aged 14 to 21. Most sought the test of their own accord and when they were healthy. In interviews, most of those tested said they intended to abstain, keep to one partner, have fewer partners or use condoms. Most had disclosed their results, mainly to partners and spouses, rather than to parents whom they did not want to disappoint. Most who had not been tested indicated that they would like to be tested in the future. Subjects said they valued the counselling aspect of the VCT, but most providers felt ill-prepared to counsel young people.

Counselling the young requires special training, particularly to reach those who have been raped, threaten suicide, plan to harm their partners, or plan to leave home or school.

4 promoting healthier behaviour

Information and education on sexual and reproductive health is critical to adolescents' development and well-being. Promoting behaviour change is essential to reducing adolescent pregnancy and stemming the HIV/AIDS pandemic.

At the ICPD, countries agreed that "... information and services should be made available to adolescents to help them understand their sexuality and protect them from unwanted pregnancies, sexually transmitted diseases and subsequent risk of infertility. This should be combined with the education of young men to respect women's self-determination and to share responsibility with women in matters of sexuality and reproduction".[1]

Programmes to provide information on sexuality also increasingly focus on giving adolescents the skills they need to make the transition to adulthood—and tend to their health needs as adults. Improving young people's knowledge is easier than helping them develop new skills. Programming is also more time consuming and expensive, as teachers and youth leaders themselves must first learn the skills—and learn how to teach them effectively. But if young people are to be expected to communicate their needs, seek out needed care and make good choices, this investment is critical.

While all young people require information and skills to abstain or stay free of the consequences of unprotected sexual relations and enjoy healthy and positive lifestyles, programmes need to target those who are most vulnerable and at risk.

BEHAVIOUR CHANGE COMMUNICATION The various approaches intended to improve knowledge, skills and attitudes are now often referred to as "behaviour change communication" (BCC). BCC topics for young people include reproductive biology, human development, relationships and feelings, sexuality, communication and negotiation, gender issues, safer sex practices (including abstinence, delay of first sexual encounter and limitation of partners), and methods of protection against pregnancy and STIs including HIV.

Methods of delivering the information can include formal and informal education, drama and folk communications, mass media (including television, radio, newspapers and other print media, and increasingly electronic media), telephone hotlines and interpersonal communications and counselling. Using several of these formats, a single programme can reach different segments of the youth population and reinforce the messages.

---

14 BEHAVIOUR CHANGE AND HIV REDUCTION IN UGANDA Young people have played a significant role in the reduction of HIV prevalence in Uganda from its peak at around 15 per cent of adults in 1991 to 5 per cent by 2001. An increase in the age when young people become sexually active, reductions in casual and commercial sex partners, and increased condom use all played a part in the decline.

The centrepiece of Uganda's response, starting in 1986, was strong political support from President Museveni, and a multisectoral response that has involved more than 700 government agencies and NGOs in the fight against HIV/AIDS. Community actions promoted behaviour change and the empowerment of women and girls, educated in- and out-of-school youth, and countered discrimination against people living with HIV.

Community-based and face-to-face communication was key to spreading behaviour change messages. Uganda's first voluntary counselling and testing centre was opened in 1990, with follow-up support provided through post-test clubs open to all who had been tested, regardless of status.

Ugandan youth have significantly changed their sexual behaviour. In one school district in 1994, more than 60 per cent of students 13 to 16 years old reported that they were already sexually active. In 2001, the figure was fewer than 5 per cent.

Uganda, which has considerable experience with education programmes on sexual and reproductive health, hopes to reach 10 million students with a new curriculum on HIV/AIDS.

BCC activities can generate demand for reproductive health services, ensure that communities accept these services, support young people in using them, publicize their locations and offerings, and reassure young people that they are welcome. Such activities must be sensitive to the different needs of diverse youth populations, particularly to differences between young men and women in knowledge, skills, power and access.

In Zambia, HIV prevalence among adolescents aged 15-19 declined from 28 per cent in 1993 to 15 per cent in 1998. This change is attributed to young people having fewer partners and using condoms more, in response to various behaviour change activities. Supporting young people to abstain and ensuring that those who choose to have sex have access to condoms are both critical to success.

In Brazil, the percentage of adolescents reporting using condoms has grown. In 1994, only 4 per cent said they used a condom in their first sexual encounter. In 1999, nearly half (48 per cent) said they used condoms regularly. The increase has been attributed to greater awareness of STIs and HIV/AIDS, as well as of the hardships related to unwanted pregnancies.[2]

Where Adolescents Get Their Information

Adolescents report a variety of sources for what they know, or think they know, about sexuality and reproductive health. In many settings, a large proportion of young people seem to rely most on the least reliable sources—other young people or the entertainment media. Young people go to different sources for different kinds of information—the news media can be important sources for information about HIV/AIDS, for example.

In most cases parents are not the primary source of information, although young women may rely on their mothers for information about menstruation and pregnancy risks.[3] Young men rely more on teachers, health care professionals or their friends.

Misperceptions abound, and can result in risky behaviour. For example: "A girl cannot get pregnant the first time she has sex;" "HIV virus is very small and go through the pores in a condom;" "You can tell by looking when someone has HIV/AIDS."[4]

Studies of young people's knowledge, attitudes and practice find a mixture of anxiety and ignorance; overconfidence, on the one hand, that they know all about it and regret, on the other hand, that they knew too little. As they emerge from puberty into awareness of the wider world, young people are often very concerned about accidental pregnancy, HIV/AIDS and other threats to their health, but they find it very hard to raise such delicate topics.

Young women may fear that asking questions will label them as promiscuous. Young men may feel that pregnancy is a woman's concern. Young people of both sexes tend to discount the risks of sexually transmitted infections and HIV/AIDS to themselves and their partners.[5] Young people are concerned not to appear more interested in sex than they really are.

Adults are often reluctant to discuss sexual and reproductive health with adolescents, sometimes from embarrassment at raising "private matters", sometimes because they think it will encourage promiscuity or at least experimentation with sex. Parents, educators and health care professionals may lack accurate information or training in imparting it to young people. Relatively little of young people's information about sexual and reproductive health comes from these sources,[6] although a study in Germany found that 69 per cent of girls said that their information came from their mothers. Parents are a more important source for younger teens.[7]

Today's young people tend to absorb their knowledge haphazardly from family, friends and other peers, school, television, movies and the Internet. The result is widespread ignorance, partial information, mistaken beliefs and myths. The best solution, especially for older adolescents, is formal sex education. Programmes vary widely in quality, but studies have repeatedly shown that accurate information at the right time and at the appropriate age encourages responsible behaviour and tends to delay the onset of sexual activity.[8] The important features are that information is available, accurate and appropriate for the adolescent's age and stage of development. Young people want, appreciate and will act on such information.[9]

Sexuality Education in Schools

Education programmes related to sexual and reproductive health have gone through a number of changes over the past several decades, many related to sensitivity about addressing sexuality. The topic has been called variously education for parenthood (especially for pregnant teens), family life education (which has sometimes omitted sexuality aspects altogether), population education (with a wide range of contents and approaches) or, more recently, life planning or life skills education (which may or may not include sexuality).

Since the ICPD, sexuality, reproductive health, life skills and life planning have all been acknowledged as key components of reproductive health education. Gender issues, which were missing from many of the earlier efforts, now also receive priority attention.

Instruction methods have also changed, from a didactic approach to one with a greater emphasis on student participation and the acquisition of skills, particularly communication skills.

Based on a review of U.S.-based sexuality education programmes, one expert concluded that school-based programmes are most successful when they give a clear, consistent message based on accurate information; focus on reducing sexual behaviours that lead to unintended pregnancy and infection; are specific to age and culture; are based on a theoretical framework proven to change health behaviours; use teaching methods that involve students, are skill-based and address social pressures; and motivate and train teachers to participate.[10]

Teachers need to be prepared to deal with the sensitive issues surrounding HIV transmission. A study of school-based AIDS programmes in Botswana, Malawi and Uganda found that lack of time, resources and teacher training undermined curriculum-based education as well as counselling and peer education.[11] A study in Colombia found that, "teachers are often unprepared to discuss sexuality with adolescents".[12] An evaluation of a successful and now-compulsory AIDS education programme in Zimbabwe found that curricula writers and teachers needed more training in participatory techniques.[13]

A study in Mexico, South Africa and Thailand in 2000 found that students have a lot to learn about HIV and safer sex.[14] The Colombian study found that "young people tend to be poorly informed regarding their own sexuality and health including contraception, family planning and HIV/AIDS matters".[15]

Yet a recent study of 107 countries found that 44 did not include AIDS education in their school curricula.[16]

Sexuality education has great potential to reach a large audience, at least in countries where a high proportion of young people attend school. A major challenge is to expand the use of approaches and curricula that have been successfully tested on a small scale.

A common misconception among parents and community leaders is that providing sexuality education will lead young people to become sexually active at an early age. Evaluations have shown such fears to be unfounded. In the two most exhaustive reviews of studies on school-based programmes, WHO and the U.S. National Campaign to Prevent Teen Pregnancy both concluded that sexuality education programmes do not promote or lead to an increase in sexual activity among young people.[17] The U.S. study also found that HIV programmes were more likely to reduce the number of sex partners and increase the use of condoms.

---

15   **HOW SCHOOLS CAN REDUCE HIV INFECTION** Studies from Mexico, South Africa and Thailand have identified some key attributes of successful school-based programmes to address HIV/AIDS:

- Teachers need to be prepared for students with a range of sexual experiences, from those who have not yet had sex to those who have experienced forced sex.

- Strategies for negotiating or refusing sex should take into account the intermittent nature of adolescent sex.

- Courses should examine peer pressure to have sex and norms about masculinity, femininity and self-esteem.

- Programmes need to address condom use so young people who do begin having sex can protect themselves and feel confident about using condoms correctly.

- Students need to be taught to accurately assess their personal risk of infection.

- Teachers and curricula planners need to recognize that students know some things about HIV/AIDS but misunderstand or are unaware of other aspects.

- Programmes need to talk about people living with HIV and AIDS.

Still, there continues to be a debate, particularly in the United States, about the virtues of teaching only about abstinence as a means of preventing unwanted pregnancy and STIs, versus providing more comprehensive information on prevention.

THE ABCS OF HIV/AIDS PREVENTION Turning back the pandemic will require a variety of approaches incorporating both prevention and treatment. The costs of prevention—financial, social and personal—are significantly lower than the costs of treatment. An approach that has become increasingly popular, particularly in Africa, is the "ABC" approach—Abstain from sex, Be faithful to one partner, and use Condoms correctly and consistently. A fourth part of the message, "D", refers to harm reduction in areas of high drug use (either injecting drug use or recreational use of alcohol). Some also refer to ABC+, which includes the message to get tested and treated for STIs (which increase the risk of transmission of HIV in unprotected sex).

Evidence suggests that many young people are changing their behaviour as they become more aware of HIV/AIDS and how to avoid it. HIV prevalence in Uganda has been reduced, in large part because young people abstain, have their first sexual relations later and have fewer sexual partners than they did a few years ago, and those who engage in sexual activity are more likely to use condoms.

The ABC(D) message is straightforward, but social, cultural and gender norms make its implementation in some places a challenge. Young women in many cases do not have the freedom to choose to abstain or to negotiate condom use with their partners.[18]

Each component of the ABC message should be presented in a comprehensive and balanced way. Promoting abstinence alone ignores the likelihood that some young people will engage in risky sexual behaviour—for example, young men who visit sex workers or young men and women who do not acknowledge their own risk of infection and have multiple partners. Promoting condoms as providing 100 per cent protection could inadvertently encourage high-risk behaviour.[19]

PROGRAMME ACHIEVEMENTS In Namibia, girls who participated in a school course called "My Future is My Choice" were more likely to remain virgins 12 months after the programme than were girls who had not participated.[20]

In Mongolia, with UNFPA support, the Government made an explicit policy decision to support sexuality education for all, every year beginning in grade three, stressing gender as a key concept.[21] Some 60 per cent of secondary schools now teach the course. Teachers and students have given strong positive feedback, while voicing the common concern that too little time is available to spend on the curriculum.[22]

Colombia began its efforts before the ICPD: sexuality education was made mandatory in all primary and secondary schools in 1993. While the programme has faced funding shortages and teacher training delays, most schools are now implementing the curriculum.[23] A school-based programme from 1997 to 1999 increased 8,000 young people's knowledge about HIV/AIDS and changed attitudes.[24] The Ministry of Health, Education and Family Welfare, working with NGOs, has developed national tools for sexuality education based on the experience.

In South Africa, national departments of education and health have begun implementing "life skills" training in public secondary schools.[25] In Mexico, a variation of this approach, called *Planeando Tu Vida* (Planning Your Life), has been tested in secondary schools; afterwards, parents, teachers and students favoured its inclusion in the formal curriculum. Students learned about contraception and were no more likely to become sexually active than those who did not participate. Sexually active students who took the course were more likely to use contraception than those who did not.[26]

Combining school efforts with other community activities, a UNFPA-supported project in the Occupied Palestinian Territories integrated reproductive health and gender issues into school curricula, adult education, and youth education programmes. Teachers and supervisors became community advocates and youth leaders were able to generate discussion on formerly restricted topics.[27]

In countries that do not mandate sexuality education, pilot projects are often undertaken. In six primary and secondary schools in Rio de Janeiro and Recife, BEMFAM (Brazil's family planning association) helped incorporate sexuality education and STI/HIV prevention into the curriculum, including on-site counselling and referrals to clinics. The use of condoms and the number of students knowing where to obtain reproductive health services increased as a result. Communication between students and teachers and between children and parents also improved.[28]

LEGAL AND POLICY CHANGES A number of countries have recently changed laws or policies to support in-school programmes:

- In 2000, Gabon passed legislation that ensures provision of information and training to girls and boys on hygiene, nutrition, and prevention of STIs.[29]

- In 2002, Panama passed a law guiding policy on pregnant adolescents. One provision requires that the Ministry of Health train and provide information to teachers so they can advise pregnant adolescents on sexual and reproductive health.[30]

- In 2001, China enacted a Law on Population and Family Planning that provides in-school education on physiological health, puberty and sexual health.[31]

- Honduras passed a law in 2000 on equal opportunities for women, which in part, requires the Government to include population education in schools, including information on sexuality, reproduction and prevention of STIs and unwanted pregnancy.[32]

INVOLVING PARENTS Many parents do not know how to communicate about sexual and reproductive health with their children, although they would like to. A survey of Mexican parents in the late 1990s found that 87 per cent supported age-appropriate sexuality education to be taught in schools.[33] Similar findings have been reported in other countries. However, even where supportive, parents are ambivalent and concerned that the contents of education be appropriate to their cultures. Involving them in design and monitoring of these programmes can ease their concerns.

UNFPA and others have developed programmes to help parents communicate effectively with adolescents about sexuality. Family Care International and the International Planned Parenthood Federation/Africa Region have produced materials aimed at facilitating such communication; young people are encouraged to allow plenty of time, not to let embarrassment stand in the way, to show respect for parents and to learn what they can about their parents' experiences.[34]

INFORMAL SCHOOLING Where school enrolment is low or special needs exist, informal education can be tailored to a target group. For example, the Bangladesh Rural Advancement Committee established informal primary schools for rural youth aged 10-15 who have never attended school, 70 per cent of whom are girls. The programme prepares students to join regular schools. Reproductive health topics are integrated into the curriculum. Special emphasis is placed on involving parents.[35] At least 350 schools have become involved. This project has also built awareness of adolescent needs and influenced community norms.[36]

In Egypt, New Horizons involved community leaders, health workers, religious leaders and parents in designing an informal programme to communicate essential information on life skills and reproductive health to girls aged 9-20. Since 1995, more than 100 NGOs have implemented the programme in seven governorates.[37]

Peer Education and Peer Counselling

PEER EDUCATION Peer education has become one of the most common approaches to addressing adolescent sexual and reproductive health in recent years. Peer education is an approach or strategy that involves the use of members of a given group to effect change among other members of the same group. Increasingly, programme evaluations are being published documenting its impact on target audiences. Still, much stronger evidence exists on the impact on peer educators themselves in such areas as increased knowledge, adoption of safer sex behaviours and improved attitudes.[38]

In Central and Eastern Europe and the former Soviet Union, UNFPA worked actively to implement, supervise, monitor and evaluate multisectoral peer education programmes, to build the status and credibility of peer education in the region, and to strengthen sexual education programmes through life skills education. In the past two years, the project has worked with 158 initiatives in 27 countries, training 165 peer education trainees—ultimately reaching 31,000 young people while integrating gender issues into HIV/AIDS prevention. The project has utilized information technology to produce the Youth Peer Education Electronic Resource (Y-PEER) with list-servs, websites, and distance learning. Y-PEER currently links 370 peer educators from 27 countries, allowing them to benefit from convenient access to resource materials and training programmes.

In Nigeria and Ghana, the West African Youth Initiative Project used peer interventions to make reproductive health information, education, counselling and services more accessible for in-school and out-of-school young people. The project operated through grass-roots youth organizations and thus depended on community involvement. It had significant effects on participants' knowledge and behaviour, including greater condom use.[39]

In Cameroon, *Entre Nous Jeunes* was designed to increase contraceptive use and reduce STIs, HIV and unintended pregnancies among adolescents. Peer educators offered group and one-on-one activities, providing information and referrals to services. Participating youth demonstrated higher reproductive health knowledge and greater use of condoms.[40] Condom use also increased after a peer education project run by a family planning association in the Dominican Republic.[41]

In Zambia, peer distribution of condoms was compared to the provision of small-business loans to adolescents. Both activities led to safer sexual behaviours, but peer education had a greater impact.[42]

Ethiopia, which has a national HIV prevalence rate of 7.3 per cent (13.4 per cent in urban areas), has trained its first group of 60 youth counsellors to combat HIV/AIDS. They will provide counselling at VCT centres.[43]

Peer education programmes can address the gender inequality that perpetuates poor sexual and reproductive health. A study in South Africa found that programmes have the greatest chance of success if they help young people understand how dominant gender norms undermine their sexual health, and give them confidence in their power to resist those norms.[44] A project carried out by the Australian and Lao Red Cross affiliates is tackling the stigma that prevents young women from purchasing, carrying and using condoms.[45]

Some programmes aim to reduce HIV risk among adolescent girls. One, on a campus in Nigeria, targets young women who use their relationships with older men in exchange for money to pay university fees. Peer activities help them discuss the risks of HIV, the need for condom use and condom negotiation skills.[46] In southern Nigeria, the Girls Power Initiative uses participatory methods to increase female students' problem-solving skills. When meeting with a male teacher, for example, girls are encouraged to take a friend with them to avoid sexual exploitation.[47]

In Ghana, where HIV prevalence among adolescents is still relatively low (2.2 per cent among those aged 10-19), peer education programmes have successfully reached 75,000 in- and out-of-school youth, including street youth and sex workers. Participants have retained what they learned about prevention, abstinence and condom use, and have passed this information on to their friends. Outreach activities complementing peer education have ensured that thousands of street children have been immunized, counselled, and given first aid and information about their health; many have used shelters linked to the programme.

An evaluation found the programme avoided problems of turnover and low motivation among peer educators that have undermined other efforts. Peer educators encountered widespread ignorance and misconceptions about such topics as pregnancy prevention, menstruation and sexual hygiene, pointing to the need to provide information on broader reproductive issues.[48]

Young people living with HIV/AIDS can be especially effective at peer education and motivating young people to protect themselves against infection. In Haiti, the Association for National Solidarity, an organization of people living with and affected by HIV/AIDS, held meetings for young people. They reacted positively to the HIV-positive leader of the group who urged them not to have early intercourse and to remain faithful to their partners.[49]

PEER COUNSELLING Peer counselling deals with addressing the cognitive, emotional, behavioural, and social needs of individuals (and groups of individuals) similar to the peer counsellor.[50] Peer counselling is designed to prevent and address problems, facilitate positive learning and behaviour, and enhance healthy development of individuals and communities.

While peer education attempts to offer knowledge and skills needed for the target group members to make informed choices, peer counselling creates this effect by additionally challenging the socio-cultural norms through a shared personal experience. With this in mind, peer counsellors require additional skills and training, as well as continuous follow-up with their clients to build on the relationship established during the counselling period.

---

16 SOWETO PEER COUNSELLOR DISPELS FEAR AND MYTHS

Mmagokgoshi Morema, 23, is a volunteer peer educator at a Planned Parenthood of South Africa (PPSA) youth centre in Soweto. The facility has an after-school "chill room" where teens can listen to music, read manuals or talk to someone.

"A young girl may come for information about sexuality or relationships. She feels free when she talks to me rather than an older person," Morema says. "If she goes to a clinic, they think she is sleeping around.

"We teach them about positive life styles, informed choices, STDs, and that drugs kill. But we don't choose for them."

Part of her job is to dispel misconceptions. "Many girls believe that when you use the pill, you'll become infertile, or you will get cellulites. When they realize it won't ruin their body, they use it.

"Some believe that if you have sex with someone standing up you won't fall pregnant. Or if you jump, or have your fingers crossed. They don't understand the menstrual cycle, or know that on certain days in the month you can't conceive. We teach them about their reproductive parts and show them charts of male and female organs."

Parents also come to the centre. One mother thought they were teaching children to have sex. "I gave her our brochures and showed her what we are really telling them. We tell mothers and fathers that if a youth comes to clinic, it doesn't mean she is having sex.

"We teach parents how to talk to an adolescent: you don't have to scare them," Morema says. "If you tell them the truth they will understand you better.

"Most youth know about STIs but not how harmful they are. When they learn, most are shocked by what they didn't know. I'm happy because now they know.

"We teach about ABC. Many young people believe abstinence is key; they abstain. Some reduce the number of partners. Many young people come to the clinic to get condoms; they are afraid of dying. We demonstrate how to use them."

Others resist using condoms. "'You can't eat a sweet inside the plastic,' some say. But they get STDs and see the light."

Morema is part of PPSA's "Million Voices" initiative, which aims to reach 3 million young people within three years. "We negotiate with principals to get invited to talk to students. Those out of school, we recruit outside at places like supermarkets and clubs."

The work is demanding and the hours are long. Why does she do it? "I have a son," she explains. "I didn't have enough information about pregnancy. My mom told me in a scary way—'When you have sex, it's painful.' I didn't know about clients' rights. She used to tear apart my room looking for contraceptives. You have to keep a card to go to a clinic; I was afraid she would find it, so I was scared to go. Instead I used a menstrual chart; maybe I made a mistake. I was 20.

"I love working with youth; it's a passion. I believed in those myths. My goal is to remove the black clouds from their eyes. You can see it."

PEER COUNSELLING IN THE PHILIPPINES Peer counselling is central to UNFPA's active programme of support for projects promoting better sexual and reproductive health for young people in the Philippines.[51]

St. Mary's University in Nueva Vizcaya shows how a Catholic school can integrate adolescent reproductive health in its programme, despite sensitivity about the issues. Peer counsellors can be easily reached in their campus hangout with reading materials on reproductive health.

Peer counsellors in Metro Manila organized the first Love Poetry contest on campus. Students participated enthusiastically, talking candidly about issues concerning love and sexuality. In Davao City, several peer counsellors were themselves former beneficiaries of the peer-counselling project. One, Belay, left a youth gang involved in drugs and theft to join the centre's youth camp. He now uses his artistic talent to assist Kaugmaon's theatre group.

Reaching Out-of-school Youth

Reaching adolescents who are not in school remains the greatest challenge. Some programmes have found a way to use peer educators for this target group. Other promising programmes sponsored by youth organizations combine informational efforts with income-producing and micro-enterprise activities. While these groups have learned important lessons, such programmes are typically small and difficult to expand because they lack an existing network or structure.

Family planning associations in Belize and Peru succeeded in reaching out-of-school youth through a drama/dance peer counselling programme and an income-generating strategy, respectively.[52]

In collaboration with the Program for Appropriate Technology in Health, the Kenya Scouts Association developed a 72-hour family life skills programme that covered decision-making, health and hygiene, STIs and HIV, sexuality, relationships and reproductive health.[53] Scout leaders were trained to teach the lessons and to work with parents on improving communication with youth, including on sexuality. An evaluation showed that working with a homogeneous out-of-school group was more effective than mixing these young people with their in-school peers. In 1998, UNFPA supported the expansion of this programme to all scouting units throughout the country over a four-year period.

Like *Homies Unidos* (see box), Thailand's Lifenet programme aimed to build support networks and peer education skills among young people at risk.[54] The programme combined various youth activities, linked itself to other organizations in support of youth, and engaged

local leaders in overcoming negative attitudes towards young people. It worked with managers of bars and nightclubs and created educational opportunities in venues where youth spent time. Young people involved in this project eventually set up their own group, Cycle of Life, and established a newsletter, a mobile phone hotline and a drop-in centre.

Mass Media, Entertainment and Sports

Mass media can be used to raise awareness in the policy area, to inform and encourage responsible behaviour and to publicize available services in the community. Programmes use a variety of formats to deliver appropriate messages to targeted segments of the population. Media and entertainment are often effective means to reach adolescents.

Sexto Sentido (Sixth Sense) is a weekly Nicaraguan "social soap opera" that tackles such complex issues as rape, sexuality, substance abuse and domestic violence. Produced by *Puntos de Encuentro*, a Nicaraguan women's NGO, *Sexto Sentido* is the highest-rated television show in its time slot and reaches 80 per cent of 13 to 17 year olds with the message: take control of your life.[55] A nightly radio talk show and youth leadership training further address issues covered in the series.

Also in Nicaragua, governmental agencies and NGOs collaborated on the *Juntos Decidimos Cuando* ("Together We Decide When") campaign, aimed at both sexually active and non-sexually active youth and young parents. Radio, television and print messages promoted child spacing, postponing sexual relations and prevention of unwanted pregnancies and STIs. Community singing contests, street theatre, dances and concerts provided venues for local health organizations to provide reproductive health information and counselling. Condoms were distributed at bars, discos and petrol stations. Most young people heard about the campaign, and many reported taking action as a result.[56]

In Zimbabwe, radio programmes, a telephone hotline, dramas, print materials (posters, leaflets and a newsletter) and peer educators informed young people about reproductive health, and led them to adopt less risky behaviours and to attend facilities upgraded to be youth-friendly. The programme also established local youth action committees and built support among parents, teachers and community leaders. The project succeeded in reaching both urban and rural youth, sparking discussion of reproductive health topics between youth and parents, increasing the use of clinics and contraceptives and encouraging sexually active youth to have only one partner.[57]

Other successful media efforts include radio call-in shows in Cambodia, Kenya, Paraguay and Zambia; youth-prepared newspapers in Uganda and the United Republic of Tanzania; and phone hotlines in Colombia, Guatemala, India, Mexico, Peru, the Philippines and Uganda.[58] These formats provide confidentiality and can reach large numbers of youth, including those who are illiterate.[59]

MUSIC AND THEATRE When big-name musicians put their names and talent behind messages about reproductive health, young people listen. Artists against AIDS Worldwide, for example, is a network of musicians dedicated to mobilizing resources to fight AIDS.[60] In Uganda, Hits for Hope attracted audiences of up to 15,000 young people, mostly young men, for a concert series and released a song that was a hit on the country's three radio stations.[61]

In West Africa, a family planning and AIDS prevention project launched in 1995 promoted a song entitled "Wake Up Africa!"; an evaluation in 1999 found that half of the intended youth audience had heard the song, and one fifth of those reported behaviour change including using condoms or abstaining from sex as a result of the campaign.

Young people in Harare, Zimbabwe, watch "Studio 263", a television soap opera launched as part of a comprehensive programme to fight HIV/AIDS. The show highlights issues that youth face and promotes abstinence, peer support and delayed sex.[62]

A UNFPA-supported radio soap opera in Jamaica sought to debunk myths, to highlight young people's vulnerability to HIV and the dangers of casual sex, and to promote condom use and abstinence. The project was reinforced by a telephone hotline and by peer educators who taught young people condom negotiation skills.[63]

In Brazil, the NGO *Criar Brasil* (Create Brazil) launched a radio programme for adolescents in poor urban neighbourhoods in the country's interior. In 2001, the programme aired on 1,100 radio stations.[64]

Ashe (an African word referring to one's inner strength and self-respect) in Jamaica is an NGO that works to build young people's self-esteem so they are empowered to make the right choices for themselves.

18 'WHAT'S YOUR EXCUSE?' HIV/AIDS is spreading faster in Eastern Europe than anywhere else in the world. But sophisticated young people, like many adults, can give any number of reasons for not wearing condoms to protect themselves.

"I'm embarrassed," admits one tough-looking hipster.

"I like it natural," says a guy dressed in black with tattoos running up his arm.

"We trust one another," say young lovers, holding each other close.

Confronting such attitudinal barriers head on is the thrust of a new ad campaign supported by UNFPA and produced by Washington-based Population Services International (PSI).

"What's your excuse?" is the slogan of the campaign. Its tag line: "There is no excuse. Wear condoms."

The campaign, aimed at 15-25 year olds, includes ads, posters, T-shirts, television and radio commercials and condom packaging. All use dark, edgy photography and sexy, sombre models. The campaign was launched at a sports and music event at Lake Ada in Belgrade in April, with some 100,000 young people attending, and in Sofia, Bulgaria, in May. It will also reach Bosnia and Herzegovina.

"I do what I want, but I know what I'm doing" is the slogan of another UNFPA-supported campaign to promote safer behaviour among Albanian youth.

Convincing young people to avoid risky sexual behaviour is UNFPA's priority focus for the region. "Right now the window of opportunity in Eastern Europe is closing and HIV is reaching epidemic proportions," says Dr. Aleksandar Bodiroza, an adoles-cent reproductive health and HIV/AIDS specialist for UNFPA. "By focusing on and bringing to scale behaviour change interventions, we may be able to save hundreds of thousands of young lives." Currently only 40 per cent of in-school and 3 per cent of out-of-school youths in the region are reached by behaviour change programmes.

Marketing campaigns like "What's Your Excuse?" represent one behaviour change strategy. Peer education—getting trained and credible young people to talk to one another—is another. Making sure that "youth-friendly" reproductive health services are available is the third part of the comprehensive approach that UNFPA supports to prevent the spread of sexually transmitted infections including HIV/AIDS.

It has performed "Vibes in a World of Sexuality", its play about personal development through peer education around the island and the world.[65] Ashe's performance challenges cultural taboos against discussions of sexuality among young people.

NEW INFORMATION TECHNOLOGIES Interactive computer programmes and the Internet appeal to young people and provide a confidential means to obtain information, and in some cases to provide counselling. While this technology is not yet widely available everywhere in the developing world, its use is increasing in many adolescent sexual and reproductive health programmes.

Western Hemisphere Region affiliates of the International Planned Parenthood Federation (IPPF) have used cyber centres, web sites, interactive multimedia CD-ROM programmes and e-mail counselling services. In Chile, a CD-ROM focuses on male roles and gender-based violence. In El Salvador, a cyber centre offers low-cost Internet access. In Guatemala, microchip technology was used to create a virtual baby adoption programme, "Baby Think It Over", that teaches the burden of parenthood.[66]

An evaluation of activities in Chile, El Salvador, Guatemala and Peru found these technologies were effective in informing urban middle-class young people about sexual and reproductive health and in changing attitudes about gender roles, but had less impact among other groups with greater information and counselling needs. It recommended linking the technology to service opportunities and involving youth in designing activities.[67]

In 2002, young women from around the world participated in an online discussion about HIV/AIDS and human rights, organized by the United Nations Development Fund for Women (UNIFEM) and the Association for Women's Rights; the exchange resulted in a booklet, "Act Now: A Resource Guide for Young Women on HIV/AIDS".[68]

The International Planned Parenthood Federation and the BBC World Service cosponsored "Sexwise", a web site with information on reproductive and sexual health in 22 languages.[69]

The Dutch National Commission for International Cooperation and Sustainable Development (NCDO) has linked 15-year-old students in schools in Argentina, Lebanon, Macedonia, the Netherlands, South Africa, Uganda and Zambia in a seven-week, Internet-based programme that examines what they know about AIDS and develops responses to the pandemic.[70]

Advocates for Youth and IPPF maintain an Internet site called Youth Shakers as an interactive resource for

---

19 YOUTH BATTLE STIs IN VIRTUAL UNIVERSE *An intergalactic war is raging. Your mission as a member of the Earth Confederation is to annihilate the creatures living on Itesius, the planet of sexually transmitted infections. The foe will be exterminated only if you correctly answer a series of questions about the transmission and symptoms of STIs and HIV/AIDS, and how to prevent them.*

This is Venerix, a computer game on STIs and HIV/AIDS that has become highly popular among Romanian youth in only a few months. It was created by the Youth for Youth Foundation, established in 1991 to enable young people to adopt healthy lifestyles and responsible behaviour.

Recognizing that young Romanians spend a lot of time navigating the Internet or playing strategy or quest computer games, the foundation created Venerix to supplement its in-school family life education programme, which teaches participants how to communicate with their peers, to make responsible decisions and how to say no, to cope with peer pressure and to use a condom and other contraceptive methods.

To make the game available to as many young people as possible, they put it on a web site, www.venerix.ro, where it can be easily downloaded. The foundation simultaneously launched an intensive game promotion campaign in secondary schools and Internet cafes.

The site is continuously improved to ensure it is dynamic and interactive. A forum and chat for discussions, flash games and a trivia game on sexual and reproductive health have been added. Last year the site attracted some 135,000 visitors.

---

peer educators throughout the world to exchange ideas, to report on emerging activities and to improve their operations.[71]

SPORTS Sports are an important avenue for reaching youth, particularly young men. In Africa, sports organizations started the Caring Understanding Partners Initiative in 1996 to promote STI and HIV/AIDS prevention, family planning and child immunization through organized sports events.[72] Other campaigns, including "Break the Silence: Talk about AIDS" in 1999 in Kenya and "Play for Life" in 2002 in Burkina Faso, Ghana, Mali and Nigeria, have successfully reached young men with lifesaving messages. Sports figures such as football star Ronaldo in Brazil and U.S. basketball player Magic Johnson have played an important role in getting messages about HIV/AIDS to young people.

5 meeting reproductive health service needs

Widespread adolescent pregnancy and childbearing, with their accompanying risks, pose a serious public health concern, and also contribute to rapid population growth in many countries. Young people additionally face high rates of sexually transmitted infections and HIV/AIDS. This underscores the need for far greater access to youth-friendly reproductive and sexual health services. Services should be provided in a gender sensitive, youth appropriate way, as part of coordinated development efforts.

Young people are often discouraged from seeking reproductive health services because of disapproval by providers and the community, as well as their own uncertainty and lack of knowledge. Countering this calls for a variety of interventions: improving the policy climate; fostering community support; addressing adolescents' needs for information and skills; and establishing responsive, age-sensitive services.

Designing programmes that can do all this, be financially sustainable and expand in scale is a major challenge. Success depends on government leadership and implementation, positive policies and laws, and the effective use of existing networks of public health facilities, schools, and other community organizations to reach a majority of the youth population.

Establishing youth-friendly services is an urgent priority.

Early Pregnancy

Pregnancy is a leading cause of death for young women aged 15 to 19 worldwide, with complications of childbirth and unsafe abortion being the major factors.[1] For both physiological and social reasons, women in this age group are twice as likely to die in childbirth as those in their twenties. Girls under age 15 are five times as likely to die as those in their twenties.[2]

Girls who are not fully developed physically encounter difficulties in sex, pregnancy and labour. Obstructed labour is especially common among young women giving birth for the first time. In Ethiopia, one study found that obstructed labour accounted for 46 per cent of maternal deaths.[3]

Worldwide, some 14 million women and girls between ages 15 and 19—both married and unmarried—give birth each year.[4] Women who start having children in adolescence tend to have more children overall and at shorter intervals than those who start later.[5]

In Bangladesh, more than half of all women have their first child by age 19.[6] In other developing countries, between one quarter and one half of all young women give birth before turning 18.[7] African countries have the highest levels of adolescent fertility and the largest variation in rates compared with other areas.[8]

In East Asia, increases in age at marriage and low incidence of premarital sexual activity have resulted in low levels of childbearing among adolescents.[9]

UNSAFE ABORTION Young women aged 15-19 account for at least one fourth of the estimated 20 million unsafe abortions performed each year, which result in some 78,000 deaths.[10] Adolescents disproportionately resort to unsafe abortion due to the limited availability and high cost of quality medical abortion procedures and because they have more unwanted pregnancies than older women.[11]

OBSTETRIC FISTULA For every woman who dies in childbirth, some 15 to 30 survive but suffer chronic disabilities, the most devastating of which is obstetric fistula. Fistula is an injury to a woman's birth canal that leaves her leaking urine and/or faeces. Young women under age 20 are especially prone to developing fistulas if they cannot get a Caesarean section during prolonged obstructed labour. Prevalence is highest in impoverished communities in Africa and Asia. Causes include early childbearing, poverty, malnutrition, lack of education and limited access to emergency obstetric care. It is estimated that three to four women develop fistulas for every 1,000 live births in areas with high maternal mortality rates.[12]

Unmet Need for Family Planning

Around the world, many sexually active young people who want to avoid pregnancy are not using modern contraceptive methods for various reasons, including a lack of access to services or disapproval by health providers. Evidence of this "unmet need" for family planning services is often indirect, particularly for unmarried adolescents, making it difficult to quantify.

In surveys of reproductive health attitudes and practice, those with an unmet need for family planning are women and men who say they want no more children or want to delay their next birth by more than two years, but are not practising contraception. Those who want no more children have an unmet need for limiting; those who want to delay their next birth have unmet need for spacing.[13]

A significant portion of unmet need is indicated by the high levels of abortion among young women, as reported in surveys and inferred from hospitalizations after unsafe abortions, as well as by estimates of out-of-wedlock pregnancies and young women's reports to interviewers that their first or second births took place earlier than they desired.

Among young people, most of this unmet need is for spacing and prevention. In most societies, childbearing after marriage is expected and nearly universal, and most newly married young people want to begin childbearing soon after marriage.

Demographic and Health Surveys in 45 countries in the last five years indicate the proportion of young people using family planning and their levels of unmet need.[14] (See Figure 5.) Surveys in sub-Saharan Africa, Central Asia and Latin America often include all women 15-19 years of age. In other regions, nearly all countries have only conducted surveys of ever-married women. This makes the results not strictly comparable, but the overall finding of high levels of unmet need is clear.

In Latin America and the Caribbean an average of 35 per cent of sexually active teens over age 15 use family planning, in sub-Saharan Africa fewer than one fifth do so.[15] As expected, both demand for and use of spacing methods far exceed those for limiting births.

The proportion of total demand (i.e., unmet need plus use) being met varies significantly, ranging from 71 per cent in Central Asia to less than one third in sub-Saharan Africa, with other regions between 45 and 55 per cent.[16]

Data from 94 surveys in 69 countries over the past decade indicate that, on average, unmet spacing needs of young people are 2.3 times higher than those of the adult population as a whole. As overall unmet need declines, the gap is even greater. Young people's needs are last to be addressed.

In sub-Saharan Africa, on average, 35.7 per cent of teenage women want to delay their next birth; in a few countries, more than half want to.[17] The regional average for meeting these spacing desires is only 30 per cent.

---

20 **FISTULAS AND EARLY CHILD-BEARING** Millions of young women get pregnant each year, before their bodies have fully matured, increasing their risk of complications during childbirth. Obstetric fistula is the most devastating disability that can happen to a young woman who survives a difficult childbirth.

During obstructed labour, the prolonged pressure of the baby's head against the mother's pelvis cuts off the blood supply to the soft tissues surrounding her bladder, rectum and vagina. The injured tissue then rots away, leaving a hole, or fistula. The baby usually dies and the woman is left with humiliating, chronic incontinence. She may also suffer from frequent bladder infections, ulceration of the genital area and nerve damage to her legs.

The results are life shattering. Rather than being comforted for the loss of her child, she is often rejected by her husband, shunned by her community and blamed for her condition. While some women receive support from their families, others are forced to beg for a living. Surgical repair has up to a 90 per cent success rate and women can usually have more children. Sadly, most poor women are either unaware that surgery is available, or cannot access or afford it.

Until now, it was estimated that 2 million women were living with fistulas worldwide. However, a new report by UNFPA and EngenderHealth indicates that these figures are too low. The report maps the occurrence of fistula in nine African countries and indicates that there could be as many as 1 million women living with fistula in Nigeria alone.

UNFPA is working with partners to prevent and treat fistula in Africa and Asia. In Chad, for example, 150 women underwent fistula surgery through UNFPA support. Fistula was once common throughout the world, but has been eradicated in areas such as Europe and North America through improved obstetric care. Obstetric fistulas are virtually unknown in places where early marriage is discouraged, young women are educated about their bodies and skilled medical care—including emergency referrals—is provided at childbirth.

Figure 5: Unmet Need (UMN) and Use of Family Planning, Ages 15-19, by Region

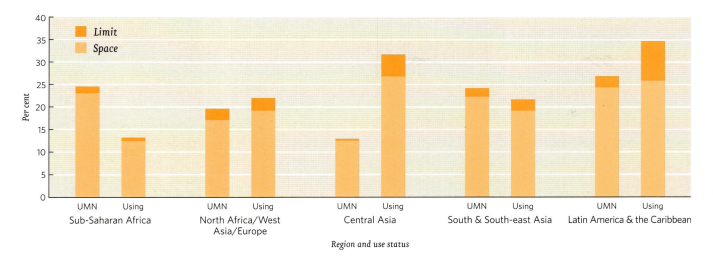

Region and use status

In North Africa, West Asia and Europe, roughly half of the demand for spacing and more than 55 per cent of all demand is being met.[18] In Central Asia more than two thirds of demand was satisfied, but one eighth of teens over 15 still express an unmet need to space their births. The few South and South-east Asian countries studied are meeting less than half of the total demand for family planning among teens but more than half of the spacing needs.

In Latin America and the Caribbean, the region with the highest demand for family planning—more than two thirds of older teens want to limit or space their fertility—unmet demand for spacing among 15-19 year olds exceeds 24 per cent. More than half of the total demand is satisfied, nearly 60 per cent excluding Haiti, the region's least-developed country.

Regional and national differences in meeting demands for family planning reflect the differences in levels and kinds of demand, marital patterns, institutional capacity and political will to address the needs of the young.

'Youth-friendly' Health Services

Since the ICPD in 1994, there has been an upsurge in efforts to provide appropriate sexual and reproductive health services to young people. These new initiatives have been developed in response to the evidence that young people often feel unwelcome at traditional family planning or reproductive health clinics, combined with an increased awareness of the special needs and rights of youth in the area of sexual and reproductive health.

Among the many barriers to services for young people are: legal and policy constraints related to age and marital status; fear of being seen, due to a lack of privacy and confidentiality; fear that they will be treated badly; inconvenient hours and locations of facilities; and high costs. In addition, many young people have a poor understanding of their own needs, know little about available services, or are deterred by shame or embarrassment.[19]

To overcome these obstacles, a variety of programme models are being used to provide "youth-friendly services" based on evidence documenting what young people want (see Box 21). These models vary from region to region.

Most countries already have a network of health facilities that can be adapted to meet adolescents' needs, especially treatment needs that are best met in adequately equipped and staffed clinics. In addition, other promising approaches have been tested since the ICPD. These include peer outreach and social marketing of condoms at non-traditional outlets (such as kiosks, bus stations, discos and petrol stations), mobile clinics, and programmes in schools and workplaces.

For the most part, such activities in developing countries have been organized only on a small scale. Larger-scale efforts in developed countries have shown that young people will use services that meet their needs—if there is community support that allows their establishment and use. New assessment tools have been developed to determine what adjustments could make clinics more youth-friendly, along with curricula to train staff on adolescents' special needs, with an emphasis on effective communication and youth-friendly counselling.

Community support for youth-friendly services is critical to their successful use. Advocacy and efforts to

Service providers:

- Specially trained staff.
- Respect for young people.
- Privacy and confidentiality honoured.
- Adequate time for client-provider interaction.
- Peer counsellors available.

Health facilities:

- Separate space or special times set aside.
- Convenient hours and location.
- Adequate space and sufficient privacy.
- Comfortable surroundings.

Programme design:

- Youth involved in design, service outreach and delivery, and continuing feedback.
- Drop-in clients welcomed or appointments arranged rapidly.
- No overcrowding and short waiting times.
- Affordable fees.
- Publicity and recruitment that inform and reassure youth.
- Boys and young men welcomed and served.
- Wide range of services available.
- Necessary referrals available.

Other possible characteristics:

- Educational material available on site to take.
- Group discussions available.
- Delay of pelvic examination and blood tests possible.
- Alternative ways to access information, counselling and services.

involve communities are therefore essential, especially in more conservative societies.

One of the most basic needs is for better evaluation of programme achievements. There are few good evaluations of projects providing youth-friendly services, and most of those were done with very short implementation periods. Good programmes take time—particularly because they depend on trained and sensitive providers who must adjust to the needs of a new generation.

REMOVING LEGAL OBSTACLES   Venezuela's 2002 National Youth Law guarantees young people the right to health care, information and education about sexual and reproductive health, responsible and voluntary parenthood without risk, and access to health services for sexually transmitted infections.[20] Also in 2002, Costa Rica and Panama amended their laws to reinforce adolescent mothers' rights to care, information and guidance.[21]

South Africa's 1996 post-apartheid constitution affirms universal rights to reproductive choice and reproductive health care. Under South African law, anyone 14 years or older has a right to receive contraception.[22]

In 2002, Argentina created a National Programme of Sexual Health and Responsible Procreation to promote adolescents' sexual health and prevention of unwanted pregnancies and STIs including HIV/AIDS, by ensuring access to information and services.[23] India in 2000 approved a population policy containing provisions on sexuality education and services for adolescents.[24]

To address the obstacles young people face trying to reconcile schooling and parenthood, Chile in 2000 and Portugal in 2001 passed legislation that ensures young parents' rights to education and guarantees greater flexibility within educational institutions to respond to the dual demands of studying and parenting.[25]

Programme Achievements

Family planning associations in various countries pioneered youth-friendly services. International Planned Parenthood Federation (IPPF) has been a leader in promoting adolescent sexual and reproductive health. In Latin America, youth centres were established, combining reproductive health information, counselling and services with recreational, vocational and other opportunities. Youth centres face some key challenges including financial sustainability and breadth of coverage.[26] Later efforts in Africa showed the same results.[27]

Many NGO efforts appear more promising although no rigorous evaluations have been conducted. Action Health International outside Lagos, Nigeria, appears to attract significant numbers of young men and women, offering reproductive health education and services, life planning skills, special entertainment activities and a quarterly magazine.[28] In Haiti, the NGO FOSREF (*Fondation de la santé reproductive et l'éducation familiale*) offers a wide range of services, family life education programmes, clubs and contests. Attendance is high and there is a large number of contraceptive acceptors.[29]

In Ecuador, a national network of health and family planning clinics run by *El Centro Médico de Orientación y Planificación Familiar* has expanded its services to better meet adolescents' needs. For example, clinic hours of operation and fees charged to adolescents have been revised. Young people participated in each stage of the effort.[30]

Jamaica's Family Planning Association is working to improve rural youth's access to sexual and reproductive health information and services, tailoring its efforts to meet needs identified by parents, local youth programmes and adolescents themselves. Its youth programmes focus on education and counselling, while also providing contraception and diagnosis and treatment of STIs, along with gynaecological care. A Youth Resource Centre offers education programmes, individual and group counselling, and social and cultural activities.[31]

In Zambia, district health managers, with support from an international NGO, are seeking to improve reproductive health services for urban adolescents and youth in clinics in the capital, Lusaka. Before launching the project, an evaluation exercise was conducted to identify adolescents' needs and increase community awareness. Parents, service providers, community health committees and adolescents all participated.[32]

Most family planning associations in Latin America and increasing numbers in Africa and elsewhere provide youth-friendly services in clinics and through outreach by peer educators. In Burkina Faso, for example, Youth for Youth supports peer educators and contraception distributors, counselling, various reproductive health services and some recreational activities. Service statistics show that 82 per cent of those who visit the project actually seek clinical services or counselling and that 77 per cent are young women (most attendees at other youth centres tend to be males).[33]

Cost and sustainability are key challenges in providing separate services for youth. Colombia's family planning association, Profamilia, long a pioneer in providing sexual and reproductive health care to youth, integrated services for young people within 13 adult clinics in mid-sized cities and small towns throughout the country. They used existing space, materials and personnel, rather than investing in new infrastructure and staff. All staff received specialized training. Advocacy was undertaken among community and governmental agencies. Adolescent visits to participating clinics increased 37 per cent during the first six months, and adolescent pregnancy tests increased by 64 per cent.[34]

Government health units at various levels have begun planning to expand youth-friendly services in public health facilities.

A UNFPA-supported project in the Russian Federation provided comprehensive assistance to youth centres in six cities and encouraged positive public attitudes about ado-

22   **ADDRESSING THE NEEDS OF YOUNG MARRIED WOMEN**

Many adolescent women are married. Early marriage is typically accompanied by strong cultural pressure to begin childbearing as soon as possible. Facing such social norms as well as barriers to reaching young women, programme planners face a challenge in trying to delay too-early first or second births.

One programme, in Bangladesh, has been successful in promoting good reproductive health among this target group. Pathfinder International has worked with NGOs for more than a decade to reach younger couples before they begin childbearing. In this programme, all newly married couples are registered and visited by a field worker, establishing a relationship with the couple and their in-laws while providing information and, when appropriate, services and referrals. As a result, contraceptive use among newlywed adolescents in the targeted areas increased from 19 per cent in 1993 to 39 per cent in 1997.

lescent access to reproductive health information. Young people helped to design these centres, ensuring that they would be well attended. Attractive factors included staff with effective communication skills, individual and group counselling, reduced waiting times, free contraception and links with other social service providers. Advocacy work with teachers and parents has been a key facilitating factor.[35]

In Jamaica, a project called "Youth.now" seeks to implement national policies and guidelines, to improve reproductive health knowledge and skills, to change attitudes and norms, and to increase access to quality services. It offers training in nursing and midwifery schools, and has established school-linked and freestanding clinics through both the private and public sectors.[36]

PRIVATE HEALTH PROVIDERS Some programmes have taken advantage of young people's preference, when they can afford it, to use private health care, which offers greater confidentiality and privacy.[37] Examples include a voucher programme in Kenya and Zimbabwe,[38] and the use of private midwives to deliver youth-friendly services in Zambia.[39] This approach may be more viable than previously thought given recent findings that young women are just as willing to pay price increases for services as older women, if services are confidential and patients are treated with respect and dignity.[40]

6 comprehensive programmes for adolescents

Since the ICPD, creative partnerships have begun in several countries to establish comprehensive programmes combining behaviour change communication with the provision of youth-friendly services and advocacy for policy change. These multisectoral efforts have built on important earlier work by family planning associations and others. These programmes are still new, but their experiences are being evaluated and shared.

There have been many successes in partnering with adolescents, their families and communities to address their development, social participation and sexual and reproductive health needs. The task of formulating integrated and comprehensive life skills programmes for more adolescents is seen as the focus of a "second generation" of programme efforts.[1]

Programmes of the second generation are based on facts, consider the diversity of adolescents, select strategies that reflect boys' and girls' differentiated experiences, and are based on human rights and youth participation principles. They involve sectors other than the health sector to support the transition of adolescents into adulthood and their gaining the knowledge, skills, and opportunities. They stress responsible decision-making, positive peer and mentoring relationships and increased power and negotiating skills.

These are some examples of projects based on the principles of the second generation:

Adolescent Girls Project

In 1999, the United Nations Foundation approved a multi-country initiative advanced by UNICEF and UNFPA (later involving WHO) to better address the developmental needs and participation rights of adolescents, with an emphasis on girls.

Thirteen countries are involved in this comprehensive, integrated approach: Bangladesh, Benin, Burkina Faso, China, Jordan, Malawi, Mali, Mauritania, Mongolia, Occupied Palestinian Territory, the Russian Federation, Senegal and Sao Tome and Principe. In most countries, all three coordinating UN agencies are involved in joint programming for adolescents (UNFPA is not active in this programme in China or Sao Tome and Principe).

Most countries now recognize that investing in and empowering women and girls is one of the most cost-effective and efficient ways to advance the development agenda. Though the specific activities in each country vary, all of the initiatives work towards some common goals to ensure that adolescent girls have the same rights and opportunities as boys.

At the core of this inter-agency programme are these fundamental building blocks:

- Creating an environment conducive to keeping girls in school through the secondary level; or at least ensure they are literate.

- Ensuring that the particular reproductive health needs of adolescents are addressed and youth-friendly services provided.

- Working with communities, including local political and religious leaders, to increase public awareness of the reproductive and sexual health issues affecting adolescents.

- Providing life skills and counselling so that adolescent girls are aware of their rights and know about available services.

- Developing vocational training and income-generating programmes for adolescent girls to increase their status, independence and opportunities.

- Mobilizing the support of decision makers at all levels to support programmes aimed at improving adolescent sexual and reproductive health.

- Contributing to equitable and sustainable development by reinforcing the capacity of national governments to engage girls in the social, economic and political life of the country.

These collective efforts are also contributing to the achievement of the Millennium Development Goals by promoting gender equality and empowering women and girls (Goal 3), by improving maternal health and well being (Goal 5) and by preventing the spread of HIV/AIDS (Goal 6).

Some examples from the field:

SENEGAL Some 10,000 girls and young women aged 15-24 from poor disadvantaged families in Dakar and Thies are the immediate beneficiaries of the project, Promoting the Empowerment of Adolescent Girls in Senegal. Through close links with communities and NGOs, girls are receiving comprehensive education, with an emphasis on gender and human rights. Perhaps most importantly, in the context of providing girls with live-lihood skills and income-generation activities, girls now have access to youth-friendly reproductive and sexual health information and services.

BENIN Some 300 adolescents and young people, aged 15-24, are being trained in communications at the Multi-Media Centre in Cotonou. They are receiving comprehensive professional training in all aspects of radio and broadcast-ing and production, computer graphics, web site design and development, photography, videography, and magazine and newspaper writing and production. It is the only centre of its kind in French West Africa.

MONGOLIA More than 150,000 adolescent girls and boys read the quarterly newspaper *Love*, produced by a team of adolescent girls in Ulaan Bator. The newspaper is by far the most popular teen publication in the country. Its pro-duction is supervised under a contract with the Margaret Sanger Center, one of the project's executing agencies. A distance education programme was implemented in cooperation with UNESCO and eight adolescent-friendly reproductive health clinics are being established across the country.

OCCUPIED PALESTINIAN TERRITORY The project Improving Adolescent Lives in Palestinian Society has mobilized local communities on the reproductive health needs of adolescents, especially girls. This has involved close collaboration with local media outlets. The project is also working to ensure that adolescents have access to appropriate reproductive health services and counselling in schools.

African Youth Alliance

The African Youth Alliance (AYA) is a four-country effort to apply proven HIV/AIDS prevention approaches on a wider scale. Operating in Botswana, Ghana, Uganda and the United Republic of Tanzania, AYA is a collaboration between U.S.-based NGOs, Pathfinder International and the Program for Appropriate Technology in Health (PATH), and UNFPA. These organizations work with implementing partners within each country: government agencies, NGOs and community-based organizations.

AYA's overall goal is to improve adolescent reproductive health. Specifically, it is designed to:

- Reduce rates of HIV/AIDS, other STIs and pregnancy among young people.
- Promote the delay of sexual debut, and, among already sexually active youth, the use of condoms and other contraceptives.
- Eliminate harmful traditional practices and forced and coerced sex.[2]

AYA uses six major strategies, each adapted to country-specific needs:

- Gaining national and community support through advocacy.
- Developing folk and mass media efforts, life skills pro-grammes, peer education and counselling, and social marketing campaigns aimed at behaviour change.
- Improving young people's access to—and the quality of—reproductive health services by institutionalizing youth-friendly services in a variety of settings.
- Integrating sexual and reproductive health into existing livelihood skills development and training programmes for youth.
- Building the institutional capacity of country-level partners to plan, implement, manage and sustain programmes and services.
- Coordinating programme activities and sharing lessons learned and best practices.[3]

All of the strategies aim to ensure youth participation, gender equity and sustainability. Implementing partners will be expected to continue the work after the five-year AYA operation ends. Management and advisory structures have been set up to facilitate collaboration among part-ners and sectors within each country and for AYA overall.

Dozens of grants have been awarded to in-country partners and activities are under way in each country.

Public and NGO clinics have been assessed and many are being upgraded for youth-friendliness. Community mobilization efforts known as Participatory Learning and Action (PLA) have been started in many communities. Life planning training has been conducted for school programmes. Young people are actively involved, offering advice on programme strategies, developing magazines and other media materials, and representing AYA at international conferences.

In **Botswana**, a Youth Advisory Committee coordinates efforts and ensures that young people participate at all levels. District and village committees—between 65 and 75 per cent youth—are charged with maximizing youth input in planning community activities. Young people are also involved as counsellors, service providers, educators, advocates and performers, and actively participate in collecting data and monitoring and evaluating activities.

Ghana's Youth Advisory Board advises the AYA country team and develops innovative ways to reach young people. In collaboration with the National Youth Council, the Board is exploring the formation of a National Youth Parliament. AYA youth representatives provide input to NGOs, international agencies and the Ministry of Health on training programmes for doctors and other health professionals to deliver youth-friendly reproductive health services.

In the **United Republic of Tanzania**, AYA and others have developed a Youth Involvement and Participation Framework to ensure programme objectives reflect young people's priorities. Young people are involved in monitoring and evaluation to determine whether programmes adequately meet their needs, and will soon participate in lobbying and other advocacy activities.

In **Uganda**, young people have participated fully in strategic planning, orientation at national and district levels, and curricula development. They work as peer counsellors and as team members in mobilizing parents and communities, in helping to design media messages, and in participating in negotiations with school administrators, local council leaders and health facility managers.

AYA's biggest challenge has been developing mechanisms for collaboration among its many partners. Expanding the scale of activities is another challenge, both organizationally and in finding evaluated programme models to build on. Partners are committed to finding solutions to structural and technical challenges, and to sharing experiences with other large-scale programmes in the field.

Adolescent Reproductive Health Initiative

The European Community/UNFPA Initiative for Reproductive Health in Asia supports projects in seven countries, closely involving international, regional and local NGOs. Adolescent reproductive health is the focus in four of the countries: Cambodia, Lao People's Democratic Republic, Sri Lanka and Viet Nam.

---

23 **LOVELIFE IN SOUTH AFRICA** In South Africa, the National Adolescent-friendly Clinic Initiative aims to make health services more accessible and acceptable, to establish national standards and guidelines, and to train health workers to provide quality services. It is a component of loveLife, a national HIV prevention programme aimed at South African adolescents. LoveLife encourages young people to wait until they are older to have sex, and when they do, to have one partner and to use condoms consistently. It is targeted at teenagers because most HIV infection in South Africa occurs before the age of 25, with young women mostly becoming infected between 15-20 years of age. With the bulk of the country's population still under 20 years, the most effective way to slow the spread of HIV/AIDS is to stop significant numbers of young people from getting infected.

The main target group is 12- to 17-year-olds, but special programmes focusing on children 6 to 12 years of age are also part of the campaign. The comprehensive sexual health strategy harnesses popular culture to promote sexual responsibility and healthy living, encourages parent-child discussion and the participation of religious leaders, while at the same time developing services that are youth-friendly.

The campaign recognizes that stand-alone youth centres may not be cost-effective or sustainable and cannot be established at the scale needed to meet the needs of most adolescents. It has developed criteria for certifying existing clinics as adolescent-friendly. Early evaluation results suggest that considerable work is needed for clinics to achieve accreditation, and to develop an operation that district and provincial health systems can maintain with minimum resources. An expansion of the programme is planned.

Organized by the Henry J. Kaiser Family Foundation, loveLife is being implemented by a consortium of four partner organizations: Advocacy Initiatives, the Planned Parenthood Federation of South Africa, the Reproductive Health Research Unit, and the Trust for Health Systems Planning and Development (HST). More information can be found at: www.lovelife.org.za.

In Viet Nam, the initiative supports eight projects with the overall goal of improving sexual and reproductive health by making services youth-friendly and promoting information and communication through NGOs.[4]

Information activities include peer education, theatre performances, youth clubs, school-based extra-curricular activities, parent groups, education in health facilities and mass media efforts. Advocacy targets community leaders, local and national authorities and media decision makers, to strengthen commitment to the programme. Implementing partners have been given technical and managerial training in service delivery and communication.[5]

Marie Stopes International is helping to provide youth-friendly services in collaboration with the Vietnamese Youth Union in Hanoi and the Vietnamese Midwives Association in Hue. These two well-attended youth centres include outreach and awareness activities to increase their coverage. A recent evaluation found that staff were professional and positive towards youth, providing a good range of needed services for free or at low cost, and that access had been significantly improved.[6]

Youth House in Hanoi will serve as a model for future efforts, including government implementation of youth-friendly services. It involves young people at all project stages; combines reproductive health information with cultural performances to increase use of services; conducts outreach in workplaces, hotels and restaurants; and collaborates with businesses and pharmacies.[7]

Geração Biz, Mozambique

In the wake of the ICPD, the Government of Mozambique made a commitment to investing in youth and adopted a National Youth Policy that aimed to increase youth participation in policy development and to improve their sexual and reproductive health. The *Geração Biz* project was designed and developed by youth, who named it to reflect their "busy generation". The project promotes behaviour change among students and out-of-school youth.[8]

The Ministry of Youth and Sports, Ministry of Health and the Ministry of Education share coordination and execution, involving their respective provincial directorates, NGOs and community-based organizations including youth associations. UNFPA and Pathfinder International provide technical assistance. The project began in two provinces and with new donor support has now expanded to six; national coverage is a long-term goal.

The number of adolescents aged 15-19 visiting clinics for counselling and services increased more than ten-fold in Maputo following the establishment of youth-friendly services; the number of young men served nearly doubled. The proportional increase in young men served was even higher in Zambezia Province. Counselling and contraception are reported as the two most popular services in both areas.

Geração Biz has peer activists in 10 of Maputo's 13 secondary schools and activities in 64 schools in Zambezia. The project is helping to integrate reproductive and sexual health information into a new basic national curriculum along with a package of in-school and extra-curricular activities.[9]

Managing activities involving so many collaborators has been a key challenge, requiring clearly defined roles for each partner and a workable coordination process. Government agencies that will assume full responsibility

---

24 **'THE RIGHT TO HAVE DREAMS'** An ambitious collaboration in Panama between APLAFA (a reproductive health NGO), the Ministry of Health, nine high schools and UNFPA has changed the lives of many adolescents in five marginal semi-urban neighbourhoods. Through a combination of education, information and health service initiatives, participants have been empowered to change their thinking about their current lives and future aspirations.

"The project taught me about the importance of not getting pregnant during adolescence," says Mónica, 18. "APLAFA provided information and counselling, which also taught me about dealing with peer pressure, the importance of having good self-esteem, and proper use of contraceptive methods."

As part of the four-year effort, the Ministry of Health created five youth-friendly clinics. Staff were trained in providing sexual and reproductive health services to adolescents. The resources built by the project guarantee project sustainability and institutionalization.

Pavel became involved with the project at age 14. Five years later, he says, "It changed the way I see life. It taught that my dreams were valuable, that I had the right and the duty to make them real." Pavel now attends the University of Panama and is an active member of Panama's Network for Adolescent Sexual and Reproductive Health.

The extensive project coverage was possible due to the creation of an Intersectoral and Community Adolescent Network formed by more than 15 private, NGO, and government institutions, which has reached more than 46,000 adolescents and youth in the district of David.

for the programme need to be strengthened and their commitment, sense of ownership and partnering skills increased.[10] Outreach activities to out-of-school youth suffer from the lack of a supporting government structure and the reality that most youth organizations are small, lack staff and are not part of a larger network. The Ministry of Youth and Sports also has insufficient staff for provincial coordination.[11]

Kidavri Network for Adolescent Skills

In India, seven diverse NGOs serving adolescents have formed a network of mutual support. With support from community contributions, international NGOs and foundations, bilateral aid agencies and United Nations programmes including UNFPA, the network produces a newsletter, holds periodic strategy meetings and facilitates the exchange of knowledge and skills. Members of the Kidavri network are a mix of religious, social action, social research and humanitarian organizations, including Don Bosco Ashalayam (rehabilitating street children), the Bahai'i community (promoting communal harmony, self-empowerment and personality development), Swaasthya (serving a large resettlement colony), the Society for Promotion of Youth and Masses (implementing programmes for the underprivileged and marginalized, particularly adolescents), Prerana (providing skills training and social empowerment) and Action India (promoting women's empowerment and community development). Network members share experiences, work on common issues (e.g., evaluation, outreach and information) and promote youth participation in decision-making.

Swaasthya is succeeding in integrating rigorous social science research with participatory community action. Research has included baseline surveys of community conditions and knowledge, and qualitative research (interviews and focus groups). Community members assist in getting information about health to neighbours. Shopkeepers distribute subsidized condoms to people who request them. Young people have made entertaining and informative films that have aired on local cable television.

Part of an international network of shelters, **Don Bosco Ashalayam** provides refuge and comfort to former street children who have been abandoned or driven from their homes. Boys and girls are housed separately. They are taught reading, arithmetic and crafts and take responsibility for cooking, laundry, cleaning and building maintenance. The regular routine provides structure to lives disrupted by the chaos of the streets. Older youths continue schooling outside. There is also a telephone help line providing street youths with information, counselling and referrals to other services.

Coordination Concerns

Large multisectoral initiatives are likely to become more common if adolescent sexual and reproductive health needs are to be met effectively. The various components of programmes that involve several sectors of government need to be carefully sequenced and coordinated. Coordination authorities must be clearly delineated or project efforts will devolve into separate activities.[12] At the same time, ownership and commitment is needed in all sectors, by all partners.

Capacity is key for successful coordination. In many instances, however, new youth ministries that lack infrastructure and resources compared to well-established ministries have taken the lead in multisectoral youth projects.

---

25   **TRAINING TRAINERS TO BUILD GIRLS' CONFIDENCE**

In a refresher workshop, 23 young women between ages 15 and 22 draw and label the parts of the female reproductive system and discuss ways to use the activity for further learning. They are leaders in Prerana, a network of New Delhi youth groups, sharing experiences in training others. Each works with ten or more younger women, mostly recent migrants from the countryside, providing information about health and livelihoods and helping build their confidence to ask questions, gain information and navigate their way in the world.

Today they are working on participatory exercises; strengthening their knowledge and skills in reading, nutrition and health; and role-playing to learn to be more assertive.

From a small start and with support from CEDPA and the Bill & Melinda Gates Foundation, Prerana has expanded rapidly, broadening its mission and serving as a resource to similar efforts elsewhere in the state and the country. Over the seven years of the project, several hundred young women have participated. Many have participated in meetings held by local governments and have been sought out by national planners.

The young women's confidence and mastery of their subjects is obvious in their interactions with their families and communities. One trainer's proud mother is almost envious of her daughter's skills; she has never known such opportunity. Previously reluctant to let her daughter leave the house without a brother escorting her, she is now confident that the young woman can take care of herself as she moves freely around the community, works with neighbours and travels to more distant meetings.

The programme's success with adolescent girls led people to demand a similar effort for boys, now under way for three years.

7 giving priority to adolescents

Action to address the critical challenges facing adolescents and young people is an urgent priority if social and economic development efforts are to succeed in alleviating poverty, curbing the AIDS pandemic, and empowering women and men to create a more equitable world. Investing in programmes to meet adolescents' reproductive health needs, in particular, is essential.

As this report has emphasized, programmes have to recognize the diversity of needs, skills and social inclusion among adolescents in different cultures, varied circumstances (in-school, out-of-school, rural, urban, rich, poor, displaced) and different ages, sexes and marital status.[1] Programme efforts must be grounded in improved dialogue with communities and community support.

Policy Environment

Experience since the ICPD in addressing adolescent sexual and reproductive health concerns has shown the urgency of having supportive policies in place. Programmes dealing with these sensitive issues cannot survive in a hostile climate. Yet few countries have policies that explicitly address the information and service needs of young people. While it is desirable to have governments establish appropriate policies before programmes are started, formal policy change may coincide with or even follow programme implementation.

Advocacy efforts are critical to gaining institutional and public support for policy changes at many levels, including national laws, policies and regulations affecting standards of practice, and community customs and traditions.

Restrictive policies can harm adolescents' sexual and reproductive health by preventing them from acquiring lifesaving information and accessing services. Laws in some countries prohibit the provision of contraceptives to minors under age 16 or to unmarried women. Even where the law permits such services, some clinics do not. In other cases, fear of condemnation by the community, or parts of the community, may dissuade young people from seeking services. Parental or spousal consent requirements also restrict young people's access to reproductive health education and services.

The absence of specific laws or policies—for instance, discouraging early marriage, or protecting girls against sexual abuse and violence—can also compromise sexual and reproductive health. Policies and laws that encourage or mandate needed programmes can have a positive impact.

A basic challenge in advocacy, especially in very traditional societies, is breaking the taboo of discussing sexual issues publicly, including acknowledging that many young people are sexually active before marriage. This would bring about a healthier society better able to meet new challenges with increased communication and respect between generations. This is essential for generating understanding within the community of the need for policy changes, particularly in response to the HIV/AIDS pandemic. Communications of diverse kinds are needed, from mass media to folk performances to discussion groups.

For programmes addressing sensitive issues, high-level commitment is essential.

POLITICAL LEADERSHIP IS KEY Political commitment—at the highest levels, matched with resources and sustained over time—is crucial for the success of programmes addressing the often-sensitive issues related to adolescent sexuality. Many governments have taken years to accept that their countries have an AIDS crisis, and to recognize that the number of AIDS cases could explode within a decade unless much more is done to stem the spread of the epidemic, including caring for citizens already living with HIV/AIDS.[2]

The countries most successful in reducing HIV/AIDS are those whose leaders took the epidemic seriously more than a decade ago, including Brazil, Jamaica, Senegal, Thailand and Uganda. Other governments have more recently recognized the seriousness of the crisis and have begun to achieve results. In India, the prime minister has urged parliament to consider HIV/AIDS as the most severe public health problem facing the country.[3]

In contrast, some policies devised to combat AIDS may stigmatize young people and infringe on their human rights, such as requiring young women to wear special clothing or markings to indicate that they are virgins. Such approaches only marginalize those in greatest need of information and outreach, while not providing urgently needed skills and protection.

There is little research measuring the impact of programmes to change laws and policy, to alter cultural norms, or to foster a supportive environment with respect to adolescent sexual and reproductive health. Such monitoring efforts are relatively new, and assessment is difficult. Most evidence of successful outcomes in this area comes from case studies and reports. Further efforts are needed to improve the documentation and evaluation of programmes.

EXAMPLES OF POLICY PROGRESS Bolivia and the Dominican Republic approved national youth policies incorporating adolescent sexual and reproductive health in 1998. Both efforts depended on strong leadership from influential politicians—in Bolivia, a former first lady and a vice-minister; in the Dominican Republic, the vice president—along with organized youth involvement, support from international agencies, and successful coordination among several sectors of government.[4]

UNFPA and the U.S. Agency for International Development helped the Government of Ghana to develop an Adolescent Reproductive Health Policy reflecting ICPD goals.[5]

In Viet Nam, the Ministry of Health has developed national reproductive health standards and guidelines that include a specific section on adolescents.[6] UNFPA is working with the Government of Jordan to develop a comprehensive youth strategy emphasizing girls' life skills and reproductive health, with advocacy efforts focused on the Ministry of Education, other ministries, NGOs and school administrators.[7]

The Kenya Youth Initiatives Project trained local leaders to become advocates for adolescent reproductive health with their national counterparts, helping to raise the priority given the issue in national policies.[8]

Rights-based Programmes

There is international consensus, affirmed by the Convention on the Rights of the Child and the ICPD, that young people enjoy and are entitled to exercise basic human rights. This provides a strong basis for programmes addressing adolescent sexual and reproductive health concerns.

Increasingly, as in other areas of development, programme planners in this field are adopting a rights-based programming approach which stresses states' obligations to enable individuals to enjoy their rights, a shift away from traditional approaches that tend to emphasize the needs of vulnerable populations without fully taking into account their capacities and rights or strategies to empower them.

A rights-based approach to development recognizes that people become empowered to act on their own behalf and enjoy their human rights as they gain access to relevant information, skills and opportunities. For adolescents, this implies progressive measures to remove barriers to the realization of their reproductive health and rights, to prevent and punish rights violations, and to take concrete measures to achieve rights.

Activities that promote the rights of young people include:

- Mainstreaming human rights education in educational policies, sexuality education for adolescents both in and out of school, training programmes, and community outreach.[9]

- Mobilizing public and political commitment to policies that address neglected reproductive rights issues including early and forced marriage, sexual violence, male responsibility, and rights to sexual and reproductive health information and services.[10]

- Establishing national and local youth policies and programmes that emphasize gender equality and the rights of young people to sexual and reproductive health, and specify measures and allocate funds to fulfil them.[11]

- Ensuring the participation of non-governmental, human rights, women's and youth-serving organizations in reproductive health policy, and legislative and programming processes.[12]

- Strengthening youth groups' capacities to participate at all stages of programming, facilitating their contribution to policy and legislative debate, and to successful programme implementation.[13]

• Creating coalitions advocating for legal reforms, enforcement measures and legislative reviews to safeguard adolescents' rights, especially in critical areas such as violence, marriage, education and reproductive health.

• Ensuring young people's participation in these efforts.

Success will depend on integrating these actions with broader national frameworks for alleviating poverty in developing countries and achieving the Millennium Development Goals (see box), including reform processes such as Poverty Reduction Strategy Papers (PRSPs) and Sector-wide Approaches to Health Reform (SWAps). These national plans often do not reflect international agreements that address the rights and needs of young people.

Indicators developed to measure progress towards the Millennium Development Goals refer to young people as an important sub-population whose health and well-being should be monitored. But some advocates for youth have been disappointed by the absence of goals specifically recognizing the special needs of this commonly marginalized age group.

Mobilizing Community Support

Even where good policies and laws have been developed, implementation has been slow and difficult. Programmes addressing restrictive social norms and promoting behaviour change require advocacy efforts to gain the active involvement of communities and reflect their local concerns, values and priorities.

Community mobilization efforts target opinion makers to encourage a more favourable climate for project implementation, and also seek to involve them in programme definition and design. This is a dynamic process that aims to ascertain the needs and interests of broad sectors of the community. Community members involved in this way become agents of social change themselves, helping to minimize opposition while advancing policy and programme goals.[14]

A number of youth programmes have successfully used a community mobilization approach known as Participatory Learning for Action. PLA involves people in examining their own situations and devising solutions to the challenges they face.

A PLA in Lusaka, Zambia, was used to design an adolescent reproductive health programme including youth-friendly services, peer counsellors and community-based distribution of contraceptives.[15] In Cambodia, a PLA in a garment factory employed a large number of young workers to develop a curriculum for a workplace programme on reproductive health.[16]

In Burkina Faso, a community participation project led by a national NGO strengthened three youth associations based in rural communities. In turn, these groups engaged community members, especially youth, in designing community-based programmes to address key reproductive health issues of concern to them.[17] The result was improved knowledge of sexual and reproductive health, increased ability to discuss sexuality issues openly, better negotiation skills for condom use, and improved access to contraception.

The Bangladesh Rural Advancement Committee has built community support for adolescent development, including delayed marriage, by providing a credit programme designed in response to local perceived needs.[18]

Community mobilization is particularly effective when undertaken by networks of NGOs addressing specific social groups that can work together, share lessons and skills learned, and pool resources.

Involving Young People in Programming

To be successful, efforts to address the rights and needs of adolescents should actively involve young people in creating and implementing policies and programmes.

Adults tend to see children through the lens of their own interests and concerns. It is often taken as completely natural that adolescents should be invisible and subordinate to adults, seen but not heard from until spoken to. The challenge is to understand and address the disenfranchisement young people face as a group and as individuals.

This tendency to neglect the voices of young people is compounded by poverty and lack of access to economic resources, but also by various, interwoven forms of social neglect that exclude them from full participation in their societies.[19]

Over the past several years, a growing number of individuals and organizations around the world have come to question the treatment of young people as lesser beings. Why has it been acceptable—and in many cases legal—to beat children, marry them before they are able to understand what is happening to them, or pay them lower wages than adults for the same work?

The Convention on the Rights of the Child formally acknowledges children's rights and not just the protections they need. Article 12 insists on children's "visibility" in their own right, and states that children and young people have a right to express an opinion, and to have that opinion taken into account, in any matter affecting them. Implementing the CRC will require a shift in how people conceive of adult-child relationships, as children are more often seen as requiring protection and guidance than as having worthy inputs to offer themselves.[20]

Promoting young people's "right to their rights", a Scottish youth group calls itself "Article 12". According to their web site, "Anyone involved in 'Article 12' believes in expressing their views at every opportunity, on anything they care about. But most importantly, they believe in creating the opportunities since, let's face it, very few adults want to listen to young people."

This new appreciation of the need to take young people's views into account can also be seen in local programmes that involve young people in improving their own health and development—rather than treating them as the passive recipients of knowledge, services, or care.[21]

DEFINING YOUTH PARTICIPATION Over the past ten years, the notion of youth participation has gained ground and acceptance, moving from tokenism to active advocacy for involving young people more fully in decisions concerning them.

Youth participation has been defined in diverse— and inconsistent—ways.[22] The International Planned Parenthood Federation has gone a long way toward defining and applying a meaningful definition of youth participation within the organization. Since 1999, IPPF's governance structure has required that at least 20 per cent

27 YOUTH MAKE POLICY IN THE DOMINICAN REPUBLIC

The Dominican Republic used a participatory process to develop its National Adolescent and Youth Policy, 1998-2003. In 1996, a national youth forum was organized as part of a nationwide debate on social priorities, including youth issues. Young participants demanded the Government lay out a clear agenda for youth, and that youth participate in the policy process. With support from UNFPA and the Pan-American Health Organization, and with much input from young people, an intersectoral committee drafted the national youth policy.

Young people further called for a law to establish a cabinet-level youth ministry and devote 1 per cent of the national budget to it, legislation that was eventually passed with some modifications. "Of symbolic and equal importance," wrote one observer, "is the law's recognition of youth as a national resource and positive force. This recognition is in striking contrast to existing laws that portray young people as potential troublemakers who must be controlled or punished."

of participating decision makers are under 25 years of age.[23] Its meetings routinely include young people who are encouraged and empowered to speak. Young people produce *X-press*, an IPPF newsletter for adolescents that is full of information about rights and health.

Participation in social groups communicates a feeling of connectedness and belonging, helping young people to develop a sense of their identity. Collaboration with peers who share some of their views fortifies their ideas and values. And the sense that one is contributing—to a cause, a decision, a group—can be a crucial part of a person's development.

All of these factors are directly relevant to the sexual and reproductive lives of young people, as well. So much of what young people need for healthy development involves their relationships with others and the capacity to negotiate relationships and to make decisions.

Working in partnership with young people is often a challenge for adult programme managers, who may believe their greater experience makes them more suited to make decisions, and may not easily accept a relationship of equality that runs counter to typical adult-child dynamics.[24]

Not listening to the young can cause direct harm to young people, encourage impunity for abusers, or simply lead to the wrong decisions. Inclusion strengthens democracy, protects children better, and is a fundamental right.[25] It is also a key to progress for youth policies and programmes.

PROGRAMME ACHIEVEMENTS Inspiring examples of youth participation can be found at all levels: from the policy process; to media campaigns; to human rights advocacy; to peer education, services, counselling, and training. Young people, when called upon by adults who are serious about seeking youth input, provide exactly what is needed and enrich the process enormously. Effective national youth councils have been established in many donor and programme countries.

Recognizing that they need to make things happen for themselves, many young people have organized to improve their social, economic and political position. UNESCO lists many youth-led organizations, such as the Siberian Youth Initiative, that promote active participation in the development of youth policies, create conditions for cooperation among youth organizations and involve youth in addressing global issues.[26]

Some countries have tried to develop youth policies that explicitly involve young people and plan for their future participation. Colombia adopted a Youth Law that stimulated active participation of young people in national development issues, and pledged to respect and promote their rights.[27] Young people have been included in local development plans, and provincial youth offices have been established.

Spurred by women's health advocacy efforts in Mexico, a group of young people started the *Elige* youth network in 1996, to promote a national discussion aimed at influencing legislators and making young people aware of their reproductive rights.[28] In 2001, with support from UNIFEM, they established a network of young women activists against gender-based violence.[29]

Elige is a member of the Latin American and Caribbean Youth Network for Sexual and Reproductive Rights (REDLAC), a regional advocacy network, which promotes the rights of young people, gender equality, and access to sexuality education and services. It coordinates the voices of youth organizations from around the region for campaigns, conferences and international meetings, and supports the training of peers.

The Canada-based Youth Coalition was formed in 1999 at a meeting in The Hague to review progress since the ICPD.[30] This international group is made up of people aged 15 to 29 who are committed to promoting young people's sexual and reproductive rights and ensuring that they are given a voice in decision-making processes—particularly those that directly concern their own lives. Members are trained to conduct advocacy efforts with policy makers.

Resources

The International Conference on Population and Development agreed on the cost of a package of reproductive health and other needs for people of all ages in developing countries—$17.0 billion a year in the year 2000, to increase to $18.5 billion in 2005, $20.5 billion in 2010 and $21.7 billion in 2015. The international community would provide one third of these amounts.

In the year 2001, total expenditure was $9.6 billion. International assistance totalled $2.5 billion, less than half (44 per cent) of the commitment for the year 2000. Developing countries contributed $7.1 billion, about 63 per cent of their 2000 commitment. A few large countries account for much of this expenditure. Africa is the region with the largest share (70 per cent) of allocations coming from international sources.

The original ICPD estimates for HIV/AIDS programme costs did not incorporate costs of blood supply monitoring, testing and counselling systems or outreach to specialized high-risk populations. It also did not include secondary prevention efforts like anti-retroviral treatments (e.g., to slow mother-to-child transmission or reduce viral loads in infected populations).

UNAIDS has updated the prevention component requirements in the original package and estimated the additional resources needed for these complementary and essential components of a response to the pandemic. The estimated requirements for the interventions in the initial estimate (mass media campaigns, in-school education, promotion of voluntary abstinence and responsible sexual behaviour and increased condom supplies) have increased by $200 million to $1.7 billion. The supportive and comple-

---

28 **DUTCH COUNCIL ON YOUTH AND POPULATION** The Dutch Council on Youth and Population, a group of some 15 young people, is aiming at the realization of sexual and reproductive rights of young people as well as meaningful youth participation in this field. Since it was started by the World Population Foundation in 1997, representatives have been part of the official Netherlands delegation to several international conferences on population and development, women and HIV/AIDS, and have participated in World Youth Forums in Portugal and Senegal. In these conferences they have advocated for an open and honest approach towards the sexuality of young people. The Council uses its expertise on sexual and reproductive rights, youth participation and advocacy in workshops and awareness-raising activities aimed at young people in the Netherlands. It has also been active in efforts to establish a European Youth Network in 2004 to promote the sexual and reproductive rights of young people at national, European and international forums.

mentary costs for prevention, care and treatment raise the total to $10 billion per year.

Additional resources would be required for basic health infrastructure development, tertiary care and emergency obstetrical care.

Further resources would be needed for other population-related development goals in the Programme of Action. Among these are:

- Universal basic education.
- The empowerment of women.
- Environmental concerns.
- Employment generation.
- Poverty eradication.

Although the Programme of Action estimates did not allocate resources to the needs of people of different age groups, adolescents and youth have been a significantly underserved population.

Adolescents challenge nations, societies and families to support, welcome and respect them. Coming of age is a time to learn limits, explore potentials and test opportunities. The choices that are made early set the course for future action. Whether or not young people make wise choices depends on the examples, the education and the resources with which they have been provided. Too often societies and families are challenged or uncertain about how to meet the needs of the young.

Young people will use whatever they have been provided with to assert their identities and chart their course. There will be over 1.2 billion adolescents for the next 50 years, living in different places and situations. Not taking young people and their life transitions into account will seriously harm the young, their families, society and future generations. Appropriate investments can ensure healthy growth and development.

Costs of Failing to Act

Youth issues are part of a complex nexus of social and economic change, and must be addressed in a multi-dimensional and intersectoral manner. Poverty, and uneven patterns of economic growth—variously aided and hampered by the forces of globalization—contribute to high youth unemployment in many settings. The expansion of formal schooling over several decades has provided opportunities and challenges in a dynamically changing workforce.

Epidemiological and nutritional developments have brought advances in health for youth; new diseases, including sexually transmitted infections and HIV/AIDS, raise challenges. Changing population dynamics alter the relative priority that policy makers give to different age groups in their budgets and planning. This complicates the issue of addressing the neglected, transitional adolescent years.

Evaluating the importance of investments in youth is complicated by several factors:

- Many interventions take a long time to have an effect.
- Investments in different areas operate synergistically, so tracing causes and identifying priorities can be difficult.
- Experimental programme designs that would allow comparison of different approaches are rarely applied to many areas of social intervention (including reproductive health and community programmes) for both practical and ethical reasons.
- Youth populations are enormously diverse: strategies must correspond to their life situations (married or unmarried, in or out of school, employed or not, in intact families or not, etc.) and cultural expectations—there are no "one-size-fits-all" approaches. What is valuable in one setting, or for one subgroup of young people, may be less effective in another—even when the costs of inaction are known to be considerable.[31]

It is also difficult to estimate the actual costs of programmes[32] and their diverse benefits (particularly those beyond productivity improvements). Complicating the situation for policy makers, investments may have different

29 | **FINLAND HELPS UNFPA SCALE UP PROGRAMMES** The Government of Finland has been a leader in supporting global efforts to address adolescent sexual and reproductive health. In recent years, it has supplemented its regular contribution to UNFPA with additional financial and technical support that has enabled the Fund to document and strengthen successful programmes, and to replicate their approaches on a larger scale. Finland has also provided support for global advocacy and knowledge sharing, a campaign to eradicate obstetric fistula, provision of youth-friendly services, the development of behaviour-change communication strategies, and the participation of policy makers and youth leaders in several global and regional meetings.

benefits for males and for females. Young men might benefit more than young women from programmes addressing tobacco, alcohol and drug abuse, for example. Reproductive health investments more directly benefit women.

As we have seen in Chapter 1 (Table 3), the web of relationships among causes and effects of negative outcomes involving adolescents are complex and mutually supporting. Breaking the links of vicious cycles that capture some people and replacing them with virtuous cycles of mutual positive support often requires combinations of programmatic interventions.

Nonetheless, research in different settings provides important information about the value of investments in youth in terms of their economic consequences.

COSTS OF EARLY PREGNANCY One key arena for intervention is the prevention of unwanted pregnancy among the young and the promotion of later childbearing.

The cost of having a teenage pregnancy as compared to a pregnancy after age 20 has been estimated[33] by considering:

- Lower lifetime earnings of the mother (reflecting earlier school dropout, childcare demands affecting education and employment, and reduced job experience)—largely private costs.

- Lower tax revenues (due to mothers' reduced income or consumption tax revenue).

- Child support cost needs (early pregnancies often involve reduced paternal support).

- Higher health care costs (complications of pregnancy are more likely for early pregnancies and later health care costs for the child are higher; these costs then affect the benefits that might be provided to others if the pregnancies had been averted or delayed).

- Additional costs related to disadvantaged children (including the inter-generational impacts of reduced education, heightened risk-taking and poverty and their attendant expenses).

- Higher social support costs (reflecting demand for foster care, child nutrition programmes, food programmes and government housing).

- Social exclusion costs (acknowledging the reduced household and community support for unmarried mothers and their subsequent exclusion from opportunities).

National social costs vary depending on prevailing teen birth levels, local wages and social expenditure

---

30 | **EMPOWERING YOUNG WOMEN IN BANGLADESH**

Shahina Akter, 20, is one of some 1,100 young women who have completed training courses offered as part of a UNFPA-supported project in Bangladesh and gone on to start their own businesses. The project aims to alleviate poverty by providing skills training and small business loans, an approach pioneered by the Grameen Bank.

Her community, Bibir Bazar, decided to concentrate on dress making, basket weaving, poultry farming and raising livestock. "I joined the club out of high school and spent six months learning to make dresses and scarves," she explains. The project also supports other community development activities and a small clinic which provides basic health services including reproductive health and family planning.

Intelligent, ambitious and with a flair for business, Shahina took out a small loan and in no time had recruited another 20 girls for her dress-making enterprise. She sells her products to stores in nearby Comilla, earning tidy profits. She also trains girls in dress-making. "There are no dropouts in my class," she says proudly.

Village incomes have risen considerably as a result of the project, and women now have economic clout, can regulate their fertility, and have fewer, healthier children later than their peers in less-enabling environments.

Locals credit the project with raising the average age of marriage in Bibir Bazar from between 17 and 19 to around 24. The old dowry system has been abandoned entirely. "In this village," explains Shahina, "the girls come to marriage with their own 'dowries', earned themselves. Here we are on more equal terms with men."

Without this project, Shahina says she "would probably have married by 19, had a child already, and remained poor and malnourished."

---

levels.[34] There are two components: financial costs (direct expenditures) and economic costs (opportunity costs for alternate uses of resources and marginal effects on other expenditures).[35]

Estimates for seven Caribbean countries of annual aggregate financial costs total $3.6 million per year. Full annual economic cost estimates reach $8.5 million. Both the financial and economic costs substantially exceed the costs of delaying these births to later ages. Direct financial costs range from $28 to $262 per birth annually, depending on their locale. Annual economic costs range from $33 to $363 dollars per birth. The annual cost of averting a birth by using family planning is only around $17.

These estimates do not include the foregone earnings of children later in their lives, as these are more difficult to estimate. (For similar reasons, a wide variety of social costs are omitted.) Detailed studies in Barbados, Chile, Guatemala and Mexico suggest that early childbearing is associated with negative economic effects particularly for the poor.[36] Adolescent childbearers are more likely to end up poor than those who bear children later. This is even observed when the women compared are matched on important dimensions.

Early childbearing is associated with higher fertility, shorter birth intervals, fewer traditional nuclear families[37] and the transmission of a preference for large families to one's children.[38] These effects are not just transitory. They persist longer the poorer the girl is initially. These effects can be reduced with further education and income, but the challenge of obtaining these is heightened. Among the poor (but not better-off women), adolescent childbearing leads to lower monthly wages. And only among the poor are effects seen on children's nutrition.

Social policies need to address information and services to prevent unwanted early childbearing and to increase education and income-generating opportunities and access to quality reproductive health education and services for poor young mothers.

COSTS OF HIV/AIDS More than 50 per cent of new HIV/AIDS cases every year are among 15-24 year olds. The proportion of these among 15-19 year olds is being studied but is difficult to specify.[39] The costs of the pandemic in arrested development, lost agricultural output, lost education, excess training costs to provide for personnel losses, health facility overloads, treatment (where available) and care, among others, are enormous. The Commission on Macro-economics and Health estimated the benefits from one averted HIV/AIDS infection in a poor country as $34,600 in settings with annual average earnings of $1,000 per year.[40]

HIV/AIDS prevention, the focus of UNFPA's work against the pandemic, has been estimated as 28 times more cost-effective than highly active antiretroviral therapy (HAART).[41] Of course, a comprehensive approach to HIV/AIDS recognizes the synergies between prevention and treatment (e.g., HAART reduces the viral load, making transmission less likely) and a balance will be needed between efforts addressing health impacts and those affecting the social and institutional contexts that place people at risk.[42] Detailed local studies are needed to ascertain the particular costs and benefits of specific programmes devised for local conditions.

Few studies of the returns to HIV/AIDS prevention efforts are available. A detailed analysis in Honduras,

where HIV/AIDS prevalence estimates are low (around 0.1 per cent), calculated the benefit-cost ratio of a school-based adolescent education programme and found that less than half the costs were recovered in benefits.[43] However, the benefits vary directly with the prevalence level. In populations with 1 per cent prevalence (a far more common time for policy-makers to take notice and institute programmes) the return would be $5 for every $1 invested. In countries with a 20 per cent prevalence, the

---

31 **LESSONS FOR THE FUTURE** Programmes to address adolescent sexual and reproductive health concerns have advanced considerably since the ICPD in 1994. Sufficient experience now exists to guide programme planning and identify key tasks for the future. Some of the lessons learned include:

- Policy makers, government leaders and civil society leaders must be involved in establishing positive policies and programmes.

- Community support is needed to increase acceptance and use of youth-friendly services.

- Youth participation and youth-adult partnerships are essential for programme relevance, ownership and effective use.

- Gender awareness and equity need to be an integral part of programming.

- Increasing the legal age of marriage, supported by social mobilization for its implementation, will be one of the efforts needed to aid young people—men and women—to better satisfy family, economic and social responsibilities.

- Prevention of too-early childbearing and of STIs and HIV should be addressed together educationally and in service programmes, with an emphasis on safer sex practices and dual protection.

Some key needs for future attention include:

- Basic information about programmes, including cost data, needs to be collected systematically and made available so all can learn from disparate experiences.

- Basic programmes, such as sexuality education and youth-friendly services, need to be scaled up, especially if infrastructure exists to build on.

- Better programme models for reaching out-of-school youth need to be developed and tested.

- Models need to be tested for programming in traditional societies.

- Documentation and evaluation efforts need to be strengthened.

ratio would jump to $99 for every $1 invested. The exact returns depend on coverage levels and on programme design and implementation.

Coordinated systems of preventive activities oriented towards behaviour change—including for those out of school, outreach to high-risk groups and prevention of mother-to-child transmission—would attain even higher levels of private and social benefits. Analyses that include the additional benefits from reproductive health information programmes (beyond those related strictly to HIV/AIDS incidence) would further increase the expected returns.

In the United States, other studies of returns for efforts preventing risky sexual behaviour have shown significant benefits. A school-based HIV, STI and pregnancy prevention programme estimated returns of $2.65 per $1 expended. A second study on preventing unprotected sexual behaviour found a savings of $5.10 in resources that otherwise would have been expended because of resulting problems.[44] Another study found a return of $5.00 per $1 spent by adding efforts to prevent risky sexual behaviour in a health intervention directed against smoking and substance abuse.[45]

COSTS OF EDUCATION PROGRAMMES Estimates of additional resources needed for quality and coverage improvements in basic education are as high as $30 billion per year.[46] The benefits of education programmes are diverse and substantial. Detailed national studies produce estimates related to their programme particulars. A scholarship programme in Colombia has been estimated to produce $3.31 in benefits for each $1 in costs.[47] An adult basic education and literacy programme in Colombia has been estimated to return $19.90 per $1 in costs.[48]

These levels of return are high relative to investments in several other development sectors (including forestry, irrigation, livestock and several agricultural programmes).

Investment in education and health, including reproductive health services, bring high returns. Benefits include: lower fertility, reduced levels of STIs, increased age at marriage, greater ability to use health and nutritional information, enhanced life skills (with appropriate curricula), and improved gender equality and equity. These many outcomes directly benefit individuals, families and nations. Disentangling these components is problematic, but it is clear that the direct and indirect pathways through reproductive health are important both for the person educated and their children. Girls' education produces higher returns.

Today, more than 1.2 billion adolescents are coming of age. Their success and happiness depend on the support,

32 GLOBAL CONSENSUS ON ADOLESCENT REPRODUCTIVE HEALTH The United Nations' five-year review of the ICPD Programme of Action called on governments to meet adolescents' needs for "appropriate, specific, user-friendly and accessible services to address effectively their reproductive and sexual health needs, including reproductive health education, information, counselling and health promotion strategies". The goal is "to enable them to make responsible and informed choices and decisions…in order, *inter alia*, to reduce the number of adolescent pregnancies".

The 1999 agreement also states:

- Governments should "ensure that parents and persons with legal responsibilities are educated about and involved in providing sexual and reproductive health information, in a manner consistent with the evolving capacities of adolescents".

- "Sexually active adolescents will require special family planning information, counselling and health services, as well as [information and services on] sexually transmitted diseases and HIV/AIDS prevention and treatment."

- "These services should safeguard the rights of adolescents to privacy, confidentiality and informed consent, respecting their cultural values and religious beliefs and in conformity with relevant existing international agreements and conventions".

- "Those adolescents who become pregnant are at particular risk and will require special support from their families, health-care providers and the community during pregnancy, delivery and early childcare. This support should enable these adolescents to continue their education."

- Countries should "ensure that programmes and attitudes of health-care providers do not restrict the access of adolescents to appropriate services and the information they need, including for the prevention and treatment of sexually transmitted diseases, HIV/AIDS and sexual violence and abuse".

- Governments and donors, by 2005, should "ensure that at least 90 per cent, and by 2010 at least 95 per cent, of young men and women aged 15 to 24 have access to the information, education and services necessary to develop the life skills required to reduce their vulnerability to HIV infection. Services should include access to preventive methods such as female and male condoms, voluntary testing, counselling and follow-up."

the examples, the education, the opportunities and the resources with which they are provided. They must be empowered to make responsible and healthy choices and provided with information and services. Investing in the well-being and ensuring the participation of the world's largest youth generation will yield benefits for generations to come.

notes and indicators

Notes

CHAPTER 1

1 This summary is based on: Cohen, B. 2003. "Youth in Cities: An Overview of Key Demographic Shifts." Power Point presentation at the meeting, Youth Explosion in Developing World Cities: Approaches to Reducing Poverty and Conflict in an Urban Age, Woodrow Wilson Center for International Scholars, Washington, D.C., 20 February 2003.

2 Significant multi-national surveys and qualitative studies of young people are being undertaken by a variety of research institutions in the United States including the Alan Guttmacher Institute, the Centers for Disease Control and Prevention and Family Care International. A review of the existing literature is underway under the auspices of the Committee on Population of the National Research Council, United States National Academy of Sciences (the Transitions to Adulthood project).

3 United Nations. 1995. *Population and Development*, vol. 1: *Programme of Action adopted at the International Conference on Population and Development: Cairo, 5-13 September 1994*, paragraph 7.2. New York: Department of Economic and Social Information and Policy Analysis, United Nations.

4 United Nations. 2002. *World Youth Report 2003: Report of the Secretary-General* (E/CN.5/2003/4), para. 16. New York: Commission for Social Development, United Nations.

5 Filmer, D., and L. Pritchett. 1999. "The Effect of Household Wealth on Educational Attainment: Evidence from 35 Countries. *Population and Development Review* 25(1): 85-120.

6 This section depends on preliminary results based on six Demographic and Health Survey data sets (Bolivia, Nepal, Niger, Nigeria, Rajastan (India) and Turkey) tabulated for: Rosen, J. (Forthcoming.) *Adolescent Health and Development: A Resource Guide for World Bank Staff and Government Counterparts*. Washington, D.C.: The World Bank.

7 Differentials from the reports in the series: *Socio-economic Differences in Health, Nutrition and Population in [Country]*, prepared by D. R. Gwatkin, et al., for the HNP/Poverty Thematic Group of the World Bank. See also: UNFPA. 2002. *The State of World Population 2002: People, Poverty and Possibilities: Making Development Work for the Poor*, Figure 7, p. 37. New York: UNFPA.

8 Source for this section: Curtain, R. 2002. "Youth in Extreme Poverty: Dimensions and Country Responses." (Draft only.) Web site: http://www.un.org/esa/socdev/unyin/helsinki/ch03_poverty_curtain.pdf, accessed 6 January 2003.

9 For a full discussion of the demographic bonus, see: UNFPA 2002 and its referenced materials.

10 National variation in age structures and dynamics can be as dramatic as the diversity of challenges to development and of opportunities to address them.

11 Differentials in health and fertility are reviewed in: UNFPA 2002, ch. 4.

12 Demographic and Health Survey data analysed by the Population Council. Web site: www.popcouncil.org/gfd/gfddhs.html, accessed 1 April 2003. Note: data not collected for most countries in South and East Asia.

13 USAID, UNICEF, and UNAIDS. 2002. *Children on the Brink 2002: A Joint Report on Orphan Estimates and Programme Strategies*. Washington, D.C.: The Synergy Project.

14 Ibid.

15 UNICEF. 2001a. *The State of the World's Children 2001: Early Childhood*. New York: UNICEF.

16 See: National Center for Missing and Exploited Children. Arlington, Virginia. Web site: www.operationlookout.org/lookoutmag/why_children_run_away.htm, accessed 8 June 2003; ChildLine. London. Web site: www.childline.org.uk/Whydochildrenandyoungpeoplerunaway, orbecomehomeless.asp, accessed 8 June 2003; and Centre for Addiction and Mental Health. Toronto, Canada. Web site: http://www.camh.net, accessed 19 December 2002.

17 Volpi, E. 2002. "Street Children: Promising Practices and Approaches." WBI Working Papers. Washington, D.C., The World Bank Institute, the World Bank.

18 International Youth Foundation. 2001. *Annual Report 2001: I Want to Belong*. Baltimore, Maryland: International Youth Foundation.

19 Larson, R., et al. 2002. "Changes in Adolescents' Interpersonal Experiences: Are They being Prepared for Adult Relationships in the Twenty-first Century?" *Journal of Research on Adolescence* 12(1): 31-68; and WHO and National Institute on Drug Abuse. 2000. *Street Children and Drug Abuse: Social and Health Consequences: Meeting Proceeds, September 17-19,2000: Marina Del Rey, California*. Geneva and Washington, D.C.: WHO and National Institute on Drug Abuse.

20 WHO and National Institute on Drug Abuse 2000. p. 16.

21 WHO. 2000. *Working with Street Children: Module 1: A Profile of Street Children* (WHO/MSD/MDP/00.14). Geneva: Department of Mental Health and Substance Dependence, WHO.

22 WHO and National Institute on Drug Abuse 2000. p. 14.

23 Walters, A. S. 1999. "HIV Prevention in Street Youth." *Journal of Adolescent Health* 25(3): 187-198.

24 Leiderman, S. M. 1996. "Learning to Recognize Environmental Refugees," p. 1. Statement prepared for: Symposium No. 316, "Environmental Refugees: Anticipation, Intervention, Restoration." Annual Meeting of the American Association for the Advancement of Science, Baltimore, Maryland, 13 February 1996. For an extended discussion of population, environment and development linkages, see: UNFPA. 2001. *The State of World Population 2001: Footprints and Milestones: Population and Environmental Change*. New York: UNFPA.

25 The Population Council. n.d. *Facts about Adolescents from the Demographic and Health Survey: Statistical Tables for Program Planning*. New York: Population Council. See web site: www.popcouncil.org/gfd/gfddhs.html, accessed 30 May 2003.

26 Amin, S., et al. 1998. "Transition to Adulthood of Female Garment-factory Workers in Bangladesh." *Studies in Family Planning* 29(2): 185-200.

27 Ajuwon, A. J., et al. 2002. "HIV Risk-related Behavior, Sexual Coercion, and Implications for Prevention Strategies among Female Apprentice Tailors, Ibadan, Nigeria." *AIDS and Behavior* 6(3): 229-235.

28 UNICEF. 2001b. *Early Marriage: Child Spouses*. Innocenti Digest. No. 7. Florence, Italy: UNICEF Innocenti Research Centre. Web site: www.unicef-icdc.org/publications/pdf/digest7e.pdf.

29 International Center for Research on Women. 2003. "Research for Policy Action: Adolescents and Migration in Thailand." Washington, D.C.: International Center for Research on Women. Web site: http://www.icrw.org/projects/thaimigration/thaimigration.htm, accessed 24 April 2003.

30 Consejo Nacional de Poblacion. 2000. "Adolescent and young workers in temporary migration to the United States, 1998-2000." *Migracion Internacional* 4(11) :1-8.

31 UNICEF 2001a.

32 UNICEF. 2000a. "Children in War: Special Focus." London: UNICEF. Web site: www.unicef.org.uk/news/soldiers.htm, accessed 8 July 2003.

33 UNHCR. 1999. "Global Appeal: Programme Overview." Web site: www.unhcr.ch/fdrs/ga99/children.htm.

34 Women's Commission for Refugee Women and Children. 2002. *Fending for Themselves: Afghan Refugee Children and Adolescents Working in Urban Pakistan*. New York: Women's Commission for Refugee Women and Children.

35 Source for this paragraph: UNICEF 2000a.

36 Mensch, B., J. Bruce, and M. E. Greene. 1998. *The Uncharted Passage: Girls' Adolescence in the Developing World*. New York: The Population Council; Adams, A. M., S. Madhavan, and D. Simon. 2002. "Women's Social Networks and Child Survival in Mali." *Social Science and Medicine* 54(2): 165-78; and Kohler H.P., J. R. Behrman, and S. C. Watkins. 2001. "The Density of Social Networks and Fertility Decisions: Evidence from South Nyanza District, Kenya." *Demography* 38(1): 43-58.

37 United Nations. 2003. *Concise Report on World Population Monitoring: 2003: Population, Education and Development: Report of The Secretary-General* (E/CN.9/2003/2), pg. 13. New York: United Nations.

38 UNESCO. 2002. *Regional and Adult Illiteracy Rate and Population by Gender*. Paris: Literacy and Non-Formal Education Sector, Institute for Statistics, UNESCO.

39 UNESCO. 2 September 2002. "Statistics Show Slow Progress Toward Universal Literacy." Press release. Paris: UNESCO.

40 UNDP. 2002. *Human Development Report 2002: Deepening Democracy in a Fragmented World*, p. 10. New York: Oxford University Press.

41 UNICEF. 2000b. *Educating Girls, Transforming the Future*. New York: UNICEF. Web site: www.unicef.org/pubsgen/girlsed/girlsed.pdf, accessed 8 July 2003.

42 Partners on Sustainable Strategies for Girls' Education. n.d. "Research Data: Gender Disparity Countries." Web site: www.girlseducation.org/PGE_Active_Pages/Data/TargetCountries/main.asp, accessed 20 January 2003.

43 Caldwell, J. C., P. H. Reddy, and P. Caldwell. 1983. "The Causes of Marriage Change in South India." *Population Studies* 37(3): 343-361; Khattab, H. 1996. *Women's Perceptions of Sexuality in Rural Giza*. Monograph in Reproductive Health. No. 1. Cairo: Reproductive Health Working Group, the Population Council; and Levine, S. E. 1993. *Dolor y Alegría: Women and Social Change in Urban Mexico*. Madison, Wisconsin: University of Wisconsin Press.

44 Mensch, B. S., and C. B. Lloyd. 1997. "Gender Differences in the Schooling Experiences of Adolescents in Low-Income Countries: The Case of Kenya." Policy Research Division Working Paper. No. 95. New York: The Population Council.

45 Mensch, Bruce, and Greene 1998.

46 Caldwell, Reddy, and Caldwell 1983; Khattab 1996; and Levine 1993.

47 Data in this section are from: United Nations 2003.

48 International Programme on the Elimination of Child Labour and Statistical Information and Monitoring Programme on Child Labour. 2002. *Every Child Counts: New Global Estimates on Child Labour*. Geneva: International Labour Office, ILO.

49 UNICEF. n.d. "Child Labour: UNICEF: Building a Protective Environment for Children." New York: UNICEF. Web site: www.unicef.org/media/childlabour/factsheet.htm, accessed 7 June 2003; and UNICEF. 2000c. *The Progress of Nations 2000*. New York: UNICEF. Web site: www.unicef.org/pon00/pon2000.pdf, accessed 5 January 2003.

50 International Programme on the Elimination of Child Labour and Statistical Information and Monitoring Programme on Child Labour 2002.

51 Ibid.

52 Ibid.

53 UNFPA. n.d. "Fast Facts on Adolescents and Youth." New York: UNFPA. Web site: www.unfpa.org/adolescents/facts.htm, accessed 23 January 2003.

54 ILO. Statistical Database. Data for 2000. Geneva: ILO. Web site:

http://laborsta.ilo.org/cgi-bin/brokerv8.exe, accessed 19 April 2003.

55 Ibid.

56 UNICEF n.d., and UNICEF 2000.

57 Emerson, P. M., and A. P. Souza. 2002. "The Effect of Adolescent Labor on Adult Earnings and Female Fertility in Brazil." Draft background paper submitted to the National Research Council's Transitions to Adulthood project.

58 This relationship is complexly determined and not necessarily causal. Preferences for work and children may be jointly determined. However, early workers who leave school may not see reproductive health materials that are often reserved for older students.

59 Cohen 2003.

CHAPTER 2

1 Miller, B. D. 1997. "Social Class, Gender and Intrahousehold Food Allocations to Children in South Asia." *Social Science And Medicine* 44(11): 1685-1695; and Das Gupta, M. 1987. "Selective Discrimination Against Female Children in Rural Punjab, India." *Population and Development Review* 13(1): 77-100.

2 Leslie, J., E. Ciemins, and S. B. Essama. 1997. "Female Nutritional Status across the Life-span in sub-Saharan Africa 1: Prevalence Patterns." *Food and Nutrition Bulletin* 18(1): 20-43. Anthropometric survey measures do not show significant differences at young ages in most settings, but disadvantage need not be severe to teach and reinforce unequal gender norms.

3 Leach, F. 1998. "Gender, Education and Training: An International Perspective." *Gender and Development* 6(2): 9-18.

4 Agarwal, B. 1994. "Gender and Command over Property: A Critical Gap in Economic Analysis and Policy in South Asia." *World Development* 22(10): 1455-1478.

5 Heise, L. L., J. Pitanguy, and A. Germain. 1994. *Violence Against Women: The Hidden Health Burden.* World Bank Discussion Papers. No. 255. Washington, D.C.: The World Bank.

6 UNICEF. 2001. *Early Marriage: Child Spouses.* Innocenti Digest. No. 7. Florence, Italy: UNICEF Innocenti Research Centre. Web site: www.unicef-icdc.org/publications/pdf/digest7e.pdf.

7 UNICEF, UNAIDS, and WHO. 2002. *Young People and HIV/AIDS: Opportunities in Crisis.* New York: UNICEF.

8 This section depends highly on the work of: Mensch, B. S., S. Singh, and J. Casterline. (Forthcoming.) "Trends in the Timing of First Marriage among Men and Women in the Developing World." Paper presented at the Annual Meeting of the Population Association of America, Minneapolis, Minnesota, 1-3 May 2003. To be included in the forthcoming National Academy of Sciences publication of the Transitions to Adulthood project.

9 South America and the former Soviet countries of Asia did not have as many as a fifth of marriages to teenage women between 1970 and 1980. Their declines have been correspondingly small.

10 See: United Nations. 2003. *Concise Report on World Population Monitoring: 2003: Population, Education and Development: Report of the Secretary-General* (E/CN.9/2003/2). New York: United Nations.

11 Implementation is clearly more important than the laws themselves. More than 20 countries have increased legal marriage age since 1990 but no clear relation to the practice is yet apparent. The relative importance of formal and customary legal systems varies considerably.

12 For these analyses, following demographic convention, marriage includes all the different forms of socially recognized unions: cohabitation, consensual unions, "free unions" and marriage that is legitimated by custom, religious rites or civil law. An inclusive definition is needed for cross-country comparisons since the frequency of different forms of union varies considerably across cultures. Only heterosexual unions are included in these data sets.

13 This section uses national data and unweighted national averages for regions calculated from: United Nations. 2000. *World Marriage Patterns 2000.* New York: Population Division, Department of Economic and Social Affairs, United Nations. Spreadsheet available at link at: www.un.org/esa/population/publications/worldmarriage/worldmarriage.htm. This database includes the last available survey from 152 countries. The National Academy of Sciences analyses (see: Mensch, Singh, and Casterline [Forthcoming.]) impose restrictions that allow them to use only 117 countries, and their trend data are based on 74 countries with multiple surveys.

14 Eastern Europe averages are higher. In some Commonwealth of Independent States, nearly 4 per cent of adolescent men are married.

15 Half or more of 15-19 year old women have ever been married in Afghanistan, Bangladesh, Congo, Democratic Republic of the Congo, Mali, Niger and Uganda.

16 The Central Asian Republics and Kazakhstan average 40 per cent, South Central Asian countries approach this level, several sub-regions average at or near one third (Middle Africa, Eastern Europe, Central America and Micronesia). The lowest rates of early marriage (below 15 per cent) are found in Northern Africa, East Asia, the Caribbean, Western and Northern Europe and Australia and New Zealand.

17 These regions include Eastern, Middle and Western Africa, the Central Asian Republics and Kazakhstan and South Central Asia. Countries exceeding 80 per cent levels include: in South Central Asia, Nepal, India, Afghanistan, Bangladesh and the Maldives; in Western Africa, Benin, the Gambia, Burkina Faso, Guinea, Mali and Niger; in Middle Africa, Angola, Chad, Central African Republic, Democratic Republic of the Congo; in Eastern Africa, Malawi, Mozambique and Uganda.

18 UNICEF 2001.

19 Greene, M. E. 1997. "Watering the Neighbour's Garden: Investing in Adolescent Girls in India." Regional Working Papers. No. 7. New Delhi: The Population Council.

20 Arends-Kuenning, M., and S. Amin. 2000. "The Effects of Schooling Incentive Programs on Household Resource Allocation in Bangladesh." Policy Research Division Working Paper. No. 133. New York: The Population Council.

21 Unisa, S. 1995. "Demographic Profile of the Girl Child in India." *Social Change: Issues and Perspectives* 25(2-3): 30-37; and Hussain, R., and A. H. Bittles. 1999. "Consanguineous Marriage and Differentials in Age at Marriage, Contraceptive Use and Fertility in Pakistan." *Journal of Biosocial Science* 31(1): 121-138.

22 Sources: Singh, S., and R. Samara. 1996. "Early Marriage Among Women in Developing Countries." *International Family Planning Perspectives* 22(4): 148-157, 175; Mensch, B., J. Bruce, and M. E. Greene. 1998. *The Uncharted Passage: Girls' Adolescence in the Developing World.* New York: The Population Council; Hersh, L. 1998. "Issues at a Glance: Giving up Harmful Practices." Washington, D.C., Advocates for Youth. Web site: www.advocatesforyouth.org/publications/iag/harmprac.htm, accessed 8 June 2003.

23 Clark, S. 2003. "Early Marriage and HIV Risks in Sub-Saharan Africa." Unpublished manuscript.

24 Sources: Singh and Samara 1996; Mensch, Bruce, and Greene 1998; and Hersh 1998.

25 Ellsberg, M. 2002. "Reproductive Health Consequences of Gender-based Violence." Paper presented at "Technical Update on Gender-based Violence (GBV) and Reproductive Health/HIV (RH/HIV)," Interagency Gender Working Group/United States Agency for International Development, Washington, D.C., 1 May 2002, See: www.prb.org/Content/NavigationMenu/Measure_Communication/Gender3/Gender-Based_Violence_and_Reproductive_Health_and_HIV_AIDS_3-c.htm, accessed 7 June 2003; and WHO. 2001. *WHO Multi-country Study on Women's Health and Domestic Violence.* Geneva: WHO. See: www.who.int/mipfiles/2255/FinalVAWprogressreportforwebpagewithoutcover.pdf, accessed 21 April 2003.

26 Nepal Health Education, Information, and Communication Center and UNFPA. 1995. "Arrange the Marriage of Your Daughter After 20 Years of Age" (Item No. PO NEP 64). Poster. Kathmandu: Nepal Health Education, Information, and Communication Center, Nepal Ministry of Health. Web site: www.jhuccp.org, accessed 19 April 2003.

27 Zhu, H. 1996. "Arranged Marriages Annulled by Law." *China Population Today* 13(3): 15.

28 Chandrasekhar, R. 1996. "Childhood in Rajgarh: Too Young for Wedlock, Too Old for the Cradle." *Economic and Political Weekly* 31(40): 2721-2722.

29 The relevant projects are described on the web sites: www.myrada.org/belgaum.htm, www.myrada.org/madakasira.htm, www.myrada.org/hdkote.htm, accessed 8 June 2003.

30 Amin, S., et al. 1997. "Transition to Adulthood of Female Factory Workers: Some Evidence from Bangladesh." Policy Research Division Working Papers. No. 102. New York: The Population Council.

31 The World Bank. 2003. "Public and Private Initiatives: Working Together in Health and Education." Washington, D.C.: The World Bank. Web site: www.worldbank.org/html/extdr/hnp/health/ppi/pubpri2b.htm, accessed 21 April 2003.

32 See: Amin, S., and G. Sedgh. 1998. "Incentive schemes for school attendance in rural Bangladesh." Policy Research Division Working Paper. No. 106. New York: The Population Council; and Arends-Kuenning, M., and S. Amin. 2000. "The Effects of Schooling Incentive Programmes on Household Resource Allocation in Bangladesh." Policy Research Division Working Paper. No. 133. New York: The Population Council.

33 The World Bank 2003.

34 Greene 1997.

35 United Nations. 2002. *World Population Monitoring 2002: Reproductive Rights and Reproductive Health: Selected Aspects* (ESA/P/WP.717). New York: Commission on Population and Development, United Nations.

36 Age at menarche decreases as nutrition improves in poorly fed populations. A plateau is reached in the early teens from which further declines are unlikely. See for example and references: Khan, A. D., et al. 1995. "Age at Menarche and Nutritional Supplementation." *The Journal of Nutrition* 125: 1090S-1096S; and Whincup, P. H., et al. 2001. "Age of Menarche in Contemporary British Teenagers: Survey of Girls Born between 1982 and 1986." *British Medical Journal* (322): 1095-1096.

37 Brown, A., et al. 2001. *Sexual Relations among Young People in Developing Countries: Evidence from WHO Case Studies* (WHO/RHR/01.8). Occasional Paper. Geneva: Family and Community Health, Department of Reproductive Health and Research, WHO; and Jejeebhoy, S., and S. Bott. 2003. "Non-Consensual Sexual Experiences of Young People: A Review of the Evidence from Developing Countries." Paper presented at the 2003 Annual Meeting of the Population Association of America, Minneapolis, Minnesota, 1-3 May 2003.

38 Brown, et al. 2001.

39 Meier, A. 2003. "The Effects of Sexual Activity on Adolescent Well-being." Paper presented at the 2003 Annual

Meeting of the Population Association of America, Minneapolis, Minnesota, 1-3 May 2003.

40 This discussion relies heavily on the UNDP/UNFPA/WHO/World Bank Special Programme of Research, Development and Research Training in Human Reproduction: Brown, et al. 2001.

41 Hoff, T., L. Greene, and J. Davis. 2003. *National Survey of Adolescents and Young Adults: Sexual Health Knowledge, Attitude and Experiences.* Menlo Park, California.: Henry J. Kaiser Family Foundation.

42 Brown, et al. 2001.

43 See: Demographic and Health Surveys conducted between 1998 and 2001. Calverton, Maryland: ORC Macro. Web site: www.measureDHS.com.

44 Ibid.

45 Population Reference Bureau. 2000. *The World's Youth 2000: Data Sheet.* Washington, D.C.: Population Reference Bureau.

46 Mendez Ribas, J. M., S. Necchi, and M. Schufer. 1995. "Risk Awareness and Sexual Protection: Perceptions and Behaviour among a Sexually Active Population, Argentina." Buenos Aires, Argentina: Hospital Clinic, University of Buenos Aires. Unpublished progress report cited in: Brown, A., et al. 2001.

47 Frase-Blunt, M. 6 October 2002. "The Sugar Daddies' Kiss of Death." *The Washington Post.*

48 Brown, et al. 2001.

49 In some settings, e.g., portions of Africa, sexual relations and childbearing are part of the extended process leading to marriage. Even in developed countries historical rates of first deliveries in the first six months of marriage have been significant. See Bledsoe, C.H., and B. Cohen. 1993. *Social Dynamics of Adolescent Fertility in Sub-Saharan Africa.* Washington D.C.: National Academies Press.

50 In this case the pregnancy precedes care-seeking. It does not indicate causation or vulnerability. See: Brown, et al. 2001.

51 The largest proportion of abortions are in married women of older ages. The proportions of young girls who are sexually active can be small; in the minority who become pregnant the proportion opting for abortion remains high. See: Brown, et al. 2001. Also see: Mundigo, A., and C. Indriso (eds.) 1999. *Abortion in the Developing World.* London: Zed Books.

52 Only Kazakhstan and the Philippines report sufficient conceptions for meaningful reporting. See: Brown, et al. 2001.

53 Ali, M. M., N. Gupta, and I. da Costa Leite. 2003. "Conception and Contraception among Young Single Women: An International Comparison." Paper presented at the Annual Meeting of the Population Association of America, Minneapolis, Minnesota, 1-3 May 2003.

54 Ibid. Results are reported for 15-24 year old women. Later analyses may provide information on under 20 year olds.

55 Ibid. Only Armenia, Kazakhstan and the Philippines had the required detailed information. These data were self-reported.

56 Ibid. These included Bolivia, Brazil, Colombia, the Dominican Republic, Guatemala, Nicaragua, Paraguay and Peru. Common law unions are relatively common in the region.

57 Finger, W. 2000. "Sex Education Helps Prepare Young Adults." *Network* 20(3): 10-15.

58 Various country studies cited in: Best, K. 2000. "Many Youth Face Grim STD Risks." *Network* 20(3): 4-9; Hope Enterprises, Ltd. 2002a. *Report of Adolescent Condom Survey: Jamaica: 2001.* Prepared for the Commercial Market Strategies Project. Kingston, Jamaica: Hope Enterprises, Ltd; and Waszak, C., and M. Wedderburn. 2001. "Baseline Community Youth Survey." Unpublished final report for the UNFPA VIP/Youth Project. Research Triangle Park, North Carolina, and Kingston, Jamaica: Family Health International and Hope Enterprises, Ltd. See also: Jejeebhoy and Bott 2003.

59 Wood, K., and R. Jewkes. 1997. "Violence, Rape, and Sexual Coercion: Everyday Love in a South African Township," p. 41. *Gender and Development* 5(2): 41-46.

60 Dreyer, A., J. Kim, and N. Schaay. 2002. "Violence against Women: What Do We Want to Teach Our Teachers?" ID21 Research Highlight. Brighton, United Kingdom: ID21 Research Development. Web site: www.id21.org/Education/EgveDreyer.html.

61 United States Department of State. 2002. *Victims of Trafficking and Violence Protection Act 2002: Trafficking in Persons Report.* Washington, D.C.: Office to Monitor and Combat Trafficking in Persons, United States Department of State; and Arlacchi, Pino. 2000. "Against All the Godfathers: The Revolt of the Decent People." *The World Against Crime,* Special Issue of the *Giornale di Sicilia:* 7

62 Coalition to Abolish Slavery and Trafficking. 2002. "Fact Sheet on Trafficking." Los Angeles, California: Coalition to Abolish Slavery and Trafficking. Web site: www.trafficked-women.org/factsheet.htm, accessed 13 December 2002; and Richard, A. O. 2000. *International Trafficking in Women to the United States: A Contemporary Manifestation of Slavery and Organized Crime.* An Intelligence Monograph. Director of Central Intelligence, Exceptional Intelligence Analyst Program. Washington, D.C.: Center for the Study of Intelligence, Central Intelligence Agency.

63 UNICEF. 1997. *The Progress of Nations 1997.* New York: UNICEF.

64 UNICEF, UNAIDS, and WHO 2002.

65 Ibid.

66 Huntington, Dale. 2001. *Anti-Trafficking Programs in South Asia: Appropriate Activities, Indicators and Evaluation Methodologies: Summary Report of a Technical Consultative Meeting: 11-13 September 2001, Kathmandu, Nepal.* New Delhi: The Population Council.

67 Lowe, D. 2002. "Perceptions of the Cambodian 100 Per Cent Condom Use Program." Pp. 9-14 in: "Documenting the Experiences of Sex Workers." Draft report for the POLICY Project. Washington, D.C.: POLICY Project, the Futures Group.

68 UNICEF, UNAIDS, and WHO 2002.

69 UNAIDS. 1999. *Reducing Girls' Vulnerability to HIV/AIDS: The Thai Approach* (UNAIDS/99.34E). UNAIDS Case Study. Best Practices Collection. Geneva: UNAIDS. Web site: www.unaids.org/publications/documents/children/young/reducingcse.pdf, accessed 21 December 2001; and Royal Thai Embassy. 1997. "Children Prostitution." Washington, D. C.: Royal Thai Embassy. Web site: www.thaiembdc.org/socials/childprs.htm, accessed 21 December 2001.

70 Balk, D. 2000. "To Marry and Bear Children: The Demographic Consequences of Infibulation in Sudan." Pp. 55-71 in: *Female 'Circumcision' in Africa: Culture, Controversy, and Change,* edited by B. Shell-Duncan and Y. Hernlund. 2000. Boulder, Colorado: Lynne Rienner Publishers.

71 Wassef, N. 2001. "Male Involvement in Perpetuating and Challenging the Practice of Female Genital Mutilation in Egypt." Pp. 44-51 in: *Men's Involvement in Gender and Development Policy and Practice: Beyond Rhetoric,* edited by C. Sweetman. Oxford: Oxfam.

72 UNFPA. 2000. *The State of World Population 2000: Lives Together, Worlds Apart: Men and Women in a Time of Change.* New York: UNFPA; and UNFPA web site, "Frequently Asked Questions on Female Genital Cutting": www.unfpa.org/gender/faq_fgc.htm.

73 El-Zanaty, F., et al. 1996. *Egypt Demographic and Health Survey 1995.* Calverton, Maryland: Macro International, Inc.; and Ministère de la Promotion de la Femme, de l'Enfant et de la Famille. 1998. *Plan National d'Eradication de l'Excision a l'Horizon 2007.* Bamako, Mali: Ministère de la Promotion de la Femme, de l'Enfant et de la Famille.

74 Carr, D. 1997. *Female Genital Cutting: Findings from the Demographic and Health Surveys Program.* Calverton, Maryland: Macro International, Inc.

75 Family Care International. 1999. *Meeting the Cairo Challenge: A Summary Report: Implementing the ICPD Programme of Action.* New York: Family Care International.

76 UNIFEM. n.d. "Circumcision With Words: Fighting FGM in Kenya." Web site: www.unifem.undp.org/newsroom/documents/kenyapro.pdf, accessed 10 January 2003.

77 Boland, R. 2003. Population and Law database (Harvard University). Special compendium provided on request.

78 Tostan. 2003. "Vaccination Project Leads To Large Abandonment Of Female Genital Cutting And Early Marriage In Senegal." Web site: www.tostan.org/news-May25_03.htm, accessed 6 July 2003.

79 McLucas, S. 2001. "Stop Excision.Net: Report from Mali." See web site: www.geocities.com/StopExcision/report.html, accessed 10 January 2003.

CHAPTER 3

1 UNICEF, UNAIDS, and WHO. 2002. *Young People and HIV/AIDS: Opportunities in Crisis.* New York: UNICEF.

2 **Note:** Figures are rounded. Source: UNICEF, UNAIDS, and WHO 2002. Cited in: Lopez, V. M. 2002. "HIV and Young People. A Review of the State of the Epidemic and Its Impact on World Youth." Report prepared as input for: UNICEF. 2003. *World Youth Report 2003.* New York: UNICEF.

3 USAID, UNICEF, and UNAIDS. 2002. *Children on the Brink 2002: A Joint Report on Orphan Estimates and Programme Strategies.* Washington, D.C.: The Synergy Project.

4 Ainsworth, M., and M. Over. 1997. *Confronting AIDS: Public Priorities in a Global Epidemic.* World Bank Policy Research Report. Oxford: Oxford University Press.

5 UNAIDS and WHO. 2001. *AIDS Epidemic Update: December 2001* (UNAIDS/01.74E – WHO/CDS/CSR/NCS/2001.2). Geneva: UNAIDS/WHO.

6 Royce, R., et al. 1997. "Sexual Transmission of HIV/AIDS." *The New England Journal of Medicine* 336(15): 1072-1078. Cited in: "Youth and HIV/AIDS: Can We Avoid Catastrophe," by K. Kiragu. 2001. *Population Reports.* Series L. No. 12. Baltimore, Maryland: Population Information Program, the Johns Hopkins University Bloomberg School of Public Health.

7 Best, K. 2000. " Many Youths Face Grim STD Risks." *Network* 20(3): 4-9.

8 Luke, N. 2001. "Cross-generational and Transactional Sexual Relations in Sub-Saharan Africa: A Review of the Evidence on Prevalence and Implications for Negotiation of Safe Sex Practices for Adolescent Girls." Paper prepared for the International Center for Research on Women for the AIDSMark Project. Washington, D.C.: International Center for Research on Women.

9 Fuglesang, M. 1997. "Lessons for Life: Past and Present Modes of Sexuality Education in Tanzanian Society." *Social Science and Medicine* 44(8): 1245-1254. Cited in: Luke 2001.

10 UNICEF, UNAIDS, and WHO 2002.

11 Ibid. Data are from the UNICEF Multiple Indicator Cluster Surveys (MICS) and the Demographic and Health Surveys, 1999-2001.

12 Brown, A., et al. 2001. *Sexual Relations among Young People in Developing Countries: Evidence from WHO Case Studies* (WHO/RHR/01.8). Occasional

Paper. Geneva: Family and Community Health, Department of Reproductive Health and Research, WHO.

13 Kiragu 2001.

14 WHO. 1998. *The Second Decade: Improving Adolescent Health and Development* (WHO/FRH/ADH/98.18), p. 6. Geneva: Adolescent Health and Development Programme, WHO.

15 MacPhail, C., B. G. Williams, and C. Campbell. 2002. "Relative Risk of HIV Infection among Young Men and Women in a South African Township." *International Journal of STD and AIDS* 13(5): 331-342.

16 UNAIDS and WHO. 1997. *Sexually Transmitted Diseases: Policies and Principles for Prevention and Care.* UNAIDS Best Practices Collection: Key Material. Geneva: UNAIDS. Cited in: *The Tip of the Iceberg: The Global Impact of HIV/AIDS on Youth*, by T. Summers, J. Kates, and G. Murphy. 2002. Menlo Park, California: The Kaiser Family Foundation.

17 Brown, et al. 2001.

18 Skhom, H., et al. 2002. "Survey on Health Seeking Behaviour of Women Working in the Entertainment Sector in Phnom Penh." Phnom Penh, Cambodia: Center for Advanced Study, Pharmaciens sans Frontieres and Family Health International.

19 Brown, et al. 2001.

20 UNICEF, UNAIDS, and WHO 2002.

21 UNAIDS. 2000. *Report on the Global HIV/AIDS Epidemic: June 2000* (UNAIDS/00/13E). Geneva: UNAIDS. Cited in: Kiragu 2001.

22 Babalola, S., D. Awasum, and B. Quenum-Renaud. 2002. "The Correlates of Safe Sex Practices among Rwandan Youth: A Positive Deviance Approach." *African Journal of AIDS Research* 1(1): 11-21.

23 Jackson, J., et al. 1998. *The Jamaica Adolescent Study.* Kingston, Jamaica, and Research Triangle Park, North Carolina: Fertility Management Unit, University of the West Indies, and Family Health International.

24 Reichman, L., and J. Tanne. 2002. *Timebomb: The Global Epidemic of Multi-Drug Resistant Tuberculosis.* New York: McGraw-Hill. Cited in: *What Works: A Policy and Program Guide to Effective STI/HIV/AIDS Interventions*, by J. Gay, et al. (Forthcoming.) Washington, D.C.: The POLICY Project.

25 Thompson, D. 2002. *Coordinates 2002: Charting Progress against AIDS, TB and Malaria.* Geneva: WHO.

26 Ibid.

27 UNICEF, UNAIDS, and WHO 2002.

28 USAID, UNICEF, and UNAIDS 2002, p., 9.

29 Ibid.

30 The World Bank. 2002. *Education and HIV/AIDS: A Window of Hope.* Washington, D.C.: The World Bank. Cited in: *The Tip of the Iceberg: The Global Impact of HIV/AIDS on Youth*, by

T. Summers, J. Kates, and G. Murphy. 2002. Menlo Park, California: The Kaiser Family Foundation.

31 USAID, UNICEF, and UNAIDS 2002.

32 Ramlow, R. 2001. "Social Marketing for HIV/AIDS Prevention in Indonesia." Presentation at the Dialogue on Social Marketing and Other Commercial Approaches to Improving Adolescent Reproductive Health, Washington, D.C., 15 February 2001. Washington, D.C.: Pathfinder International/FOCUS on Young Adults.

33 Population Services International and Population Reference Bureau. 2000. *Social Marketing for Adolescent Sexual Health: Results of Operations Research Projects in Botswana, Cameroon, Guinea, and South Africa.* Washington, D.C.: Population Services International and Population Reference Bureau; Agha, S. 2000. "An Evaluation of Adolescent Sexual Health Programs in Cameroon, Botswana, South Africa, and Guinea." Population Services International Research Division Working Paper. No. 29. Washington, D.C.: Population Services International; and Van Rossen, R., and D. Meekers. 1999. "The Evaluation of the Effectiveness of Targeted Social Marketing to Promote Adolescent Reproductive Health in Guinea." Population Services International Research Division Working Paper. No. 23. Washington, D.C.: Population Services International.

34 Meekers, D., and M. Klein. 2003. "Determinants of Condom Use Among Young People in Urban Cameroon." *Studies in Family Planning* 33(4): 335-346.

35 Nyamongo, I. 1995. "Investigation into Condom Acceptability, Sexual Behaviour and Attitudes about HIV Infection and AIDS Among Adolescent Students in Kenya." Unpublished report. Nairobi, Kenya: Institute of African Studies, University of Nairobi. Cited in: Brown, et al. 2001.

36 Kgosidintsi, N. 1997. "Sexual Behaviour and Risk of HIV Infection Among Adolescent Females in Botswana." Unpublished report. Gaborone, Botswana: National Institute of Development, Research and Documentation. Cited in: Brown, et al. 2001.

37 Heald, S. 2002. "It's Never As Easy as ABC: Understandings of AIDS in Botswana." *African Journal of AIDS Research* 1(1): 1-10.

38 Sarafian, I. 2001. "Final Report on Findings: HIV/AIDS and Youth in Suriname." Paramaribo, Suriname: PAHO/WHO.

39 Best 2000.

40 FOCUS on Young Adults. 2001. *Advancing Young Adult Reproductive Health: Actions for the Next Decade.* End of Programme Report: 2001. Washington, D.C.: Pathfinder International and the Futures Group.

41 Horizons Program, Kenya Project Partners, and Uganda Project Partners. 2001. *HIV Voluntary Counseling and*

Testing Among Youth: Results from an Exploratory Study in Nairobi, Kenya, and Kampala and Masaka, Uganda. Washington, D.C.: Horizons Program, the Population Council.

42 Thompson 2002.

CHAPTER 4

1 United Nations. 1995. *Population and Development*, vol. 1: *Programme of Action adopted at the International Conference on Population and Development: Cairo, 5-13 September 1994*, paragraph 7.41. New York: Department of Economic and Social Information and Policy Analysis, United Nations.

2 Rebourças, L. 2002. "Brazil Confronts Adolescent Sexual Health Issues." Washington, D.C.: Population Reference Bureau. Web site: www.prb.org///Template.cfm?Section=P RB&template=/Content/ContentGroups/ Articles/02/Brazil_Confronts_Adolescent_ Sexual_Health_Issues.htm, accessed 13 November 2002.

3 Brown, A., et al. 2001. *Sexual Relations among Young People in Developing Countries: Evidence from WHO Case Studies* (WHO/RHR/01.8). Occasional Paper. Geneva: Family and Community Health, Department of Reproductive Health and Research, WHO, pg. 35. This section also draws extensively on: McCauley, A. P., and C. Salter. 1995. *Meeting the Needs Of Young Adults. Population Reports.* Series J, No. 41. Baltimore, Maryland: Population Information Program, Johns Hopkins School of Public Health.

4 Examples from: Brown, et al. 2001, pp. 29-30.

5 Ibid., p. 30.

6 Ibid., p. 34.

7 Federal Centre for Health Education. 1998. *Youth Sexuality 1998: Results of the Current Representative Survey.* Cologne: The Centre.

8 See: Grunseit, A., and S. Kippax, 1993. *Effects of Sex Education on Young People's Sexual Behavior.* Geneva: WHO; Kirby, D. 2001. *Emerging Answers: Research Findings on Programs to Reduce Teen Pregnancy.* Washington, D.C.: National Campaign to Prevent Teen Pregnancy. Web site: www.teenpregnancy.org, accessed 7 July 2002; and Health Development Agency. 2001. *Teenage Pregnancy: An Update on Key Characteristics of Effective Interventions.* London: National Health Service. Web site: www.hda-online.org.uk/ documents/teenpreg.pdf, accessed 7 July 2003.

9 Brown, et al. 2001, p. 35.

10 Kirby 2001. Cited in: "Sexuality and Family Life Education Helps Prepare Young People," No. 2 in a Series, by K. Katz and W. Finger. 2002. *YouthLens on Reproductive Health and HIV/AIDS.* Arlington, Virginia: YouthNet.

11 "AIDS Education Fails to Change Behavior." 2 November 2002. *East African Standard* (Nairobi).

12 Perez, F., and F. Dabis. 2003. "HIV Prevention in Latin America: Reaching Youth in Colombia," p. 85. *AIDS Care* 15(1): 77-87.

13 O'Donoghue, J. 2002. "Zimbabwe's AIDS Action Programme for Schools." *Evaluation and Programme Planning* 25(4): 387-396.

14 Stewart, H., et al. 2001. *Reducing HIV Infection Among Youth: What Can Schools Do: Key Baseline Findings from Mexico, South Africa, and Thailand.* Washington, D.C.: Horizons Program, the Population Council.

15 Perez and Dabis 2003.

16 Population Reference Bureau. 2000. *The World's Youth 2000.* Washington, D.C.: Population Reference Bureau. Cited in: "Youth and HIV/AIDS: Can We Avoid Catastrophe," by K. Kiragu. 2001. *Population Reports.* Series L. No. 12. Baltimore, Maryland: Population Information Program, the Johns Hopkins University Bloomberg School of Public Health.

17 Kirby 2001.

18 In assessing the reaction to the ABC message in Botswana, one analysis concluded that "human choices are con-strained and depend on who and where one is, especially in such emotive and important an area as human sexuality. People cannot be assumed to be autonomous agents operating in a social vacuum. It has become increasingly clear that while some may have such choice, there are many others who have no such freedom, and the position of women, whether married, poor or young, has been a particular focus of concern." Heald, S. 2002. "It's Never As Easy as ABC: Understandings of AIDS in Botswana," p.3. *African Journal of AIDS Research* 1(1): 1-10.

19 Source: Shelton, J. 29 July 2002. "Jim Shelton's Pearls: ABC Approach to Behaviour Change." Web site: www.jhuccp.org/pearls/2002/ 07-29.shtml.

20 Stanton, B. F., et al. 1998. "Increased Protected Sex and Abstinence Among Namibian Youth Following a HIV Risk-reduction Intervention: A Randomized, Longitudinal Study." *AIDS* 12(18): 2473-2480.

21 Barcelona, D., and L. Laski. 2002. "Introduction: What Are We Learning about Sexuality Education?" *Quality/Calidad/Qualité: Universal Sexuality Education in Mongolia: Educating Today to Protect Tomorrow.* No. 12: 1-5. New York: The Population Council.

22 Gerdts, C. 2002. "Universal Sexuality Education in Mongolia: Educating Today to Protect Tomorrow." *Universal Sexuality Education in Mongolia: Educating Today to Protect Tomorrow. Quality/Calidad/Qualité.* No. 12: 5-31. New York: The Population Council.

23 Smith, J., and C. Colvin. 2000. *Getting to Scale in Young Adult Reproductive Health Programs.* FOCUS Tool Series. No. 3. Washington, D.C.: FOCUS on Young Adults, Pathfinder International; and UNFPA. n.d. "UNFPA in Action: Case

Study: Critical Information: Getting the Message Out: Bangladesh, Colombia, Jamaica, Occupied Palestinian Territories, Philippines, Vanuatu, Vietnam." New York: UNFPA. Web Site: www.unfpa.org/adolescents/casestudies/case001.htm, accessed 5 January 2003.

24 Perez and Dabis 2003.

25 FOCUS on Young Adults. n.d. "Evaluation of Life Skills in Public Schools in KwaZulu Natal, South Africa: Baseline Survey Report." Unpublished summary report. Washington, D.C.: FOCUS on Young Adults, Pathfinder International.

26 Pick de Weiss, S., et al. 1998. "Family Life Education Increases Contraceptive Knowledge and Use by Mexican Youth." *Operations Research Summaries*. New York: The Population Council.

27 UNFPA n.d.

28 International Planned Parenthood Federation. 2001a. "Working in Schools: Sex Education in Brazil." *IPPF/WHR Spotlight on Youth*. No. 3. New York: International Planned Parenthood Federation.

29 Boland, R. 2003. Population and Law database (Harvard University). Special compendium provided on request, p. 10.

30 Ibid., p. 2.

31 Ibid., p. 1.

32 Ibid.

33 Pick, S., M. Givaudan, and J. Brown. 2000. "Quietly Working for School-Based Sexuality Education in Mexico: Strategies for Advocacy." *Reproductive Health Matters* 8(16): 92-102.

34 Family Care International. 1999. *Get the Facts: A Flipchart for Adolescents*. New York: Family Care International.

35 Bond, K., and L. MacLaren. 1998. "Report on Consultancy to NIPHP Partners: Bangladesh: November 29-December 14, 1998." Washington, D.C.: FOCUS on Young Adults, Pathfinder International.

36 Barkat, A., et al. 1999. "An Assessment of RSDP/BRAC Adolescent Family Life Education Program." Washington, D.C.: FOCUS on Young Adults, Pathfinder International.

37 Meeting with Centre for Development and Population Activities (CEDPA) staff, 26 April 2000; and unpublished CEDPA memos and reports.

38 Senderowitz, J. 2000. "A Review of Program Approaches to Adolescent Reproductive Health." Poptech Assignment. No. 2000.176. Arlington, Virginia: Population Technical Assistance Project.

39 "West African Youth Initiative Project: Summary of Key Findings." n.d. Ibadan, Nigeria, and Washington, D.C.: Association for Reproductive and Family Health, African Regional Health Education Centre, and Advocates for Youth.

40 Speizer, I., B. Oleko Tambashe, and S. P. Tegang. 2001. "An Evaluation of the 'Entre Nous Jeunes' Peer-educator Program for Adolescents in Cameroon." *Studies in Family Planning* 32(4): 339-351.

41 International Planned Parenthood Federation. 2001b. "Working in Communities: Youth Peer Education in the Dominican Republic." *IPPF/WHR Spotlight on Youth*. No. 2. New York: International Planned Parenthood Federation/Western Hemisphere Region.

42 "Zambia Youth Reproductive Health." 2001. *OR Summary*. No. 17. New York: Frontiers in Reproductive Health, the Population Council.

43 United Nations Integrated Regional Information Networks (IRIN). 20 May 2002. "Training for HIV/Aids Youth Counsellors Launched." Web site: www.aegis.com/news/irin/2002/IR020 510.html, accessed 5 December 2002.

44 Campbell, C., and C. MacPhail. 2002. "Peer Education, Gender and the Development of Critical Consciousness: Participatory HIV Prevention by South African Youth." *Social Science and Medicine* 55(2): 331-345.

45 Australian Red Cross and Lao Red Cross. 2003. "Youth Peer Education: A Gendered Perspective." Web site: http://archives.healthdev.net/gender-aids/msg00512.html, 23 April posting.

46 Abang, M. 1996. "Promoting HIV/AIDS Prevention on Nigerian Campuses: Students Take the Lead." *AIDScaptions* 3(3). Cited in: "Cross-generational and Transactional Sexual Relations in Sub-Saharan Africa: A Review of the Evidence and Prevalence for Negotiation of Safe Sex Practices for Adolescent Girls," by N. Luke. 2001. Paper prepared for the International Center for Research on Women for the AIDSMark Project. Washington, D.C.: International Center for Research on Women.

47 Irvin, A. 2000. *Taking Steps of Courage: Teaching Adolescents about Sexuality and Gender in Nigeria and Cameroon*. New York: International Women's Health Coalition. Cited in: Luke 2001.

48 UNICEF Ghana. 2002. "Evaluation of HIV/AIDS Prevention Through Peer Education, Counselling, Health Care, Training, and Urban Refuges in Ghana." *Evaluation and Programme Planning* 25(4): 409-420.

49 Beaujour, S. 2000. Quoted in: Colbert, R. 2000. "HIV/AIDS-Cabaret: Youth Motivated for Safe Sexual Relations." Web site: www.panosinst.org/Island/IB46e.shtml, accessed 5 December 2002.

50 Usually, one or more socio-cultural characteristics, such as age, gender or sex, as well as personal experiences, such as drug use, child bearing at an early age, HIV status, etc., are shared by both the peer counsellor and the client.

51 This section is based on reporting by Francisco Llaguno, who visited UNFPA-supported projects throughout the Philippines in early 2003.

52 Kohn, D. 2002. "Working with Out-of-school Youth in Belize and Peru." *Siecus Report: Sexual Health Issues Worldwide* 30(5).

53 Kahuthia, G., and S. Radeny. 1999. "PATH, Kenya: Using Scouting as a Vehicle for Reaching Out-of School Youth." FOCUS Project Highlights. Washington, D.C.: FOCUS on Young Adults. Web site: www.fhi.org/en/youth/youthnet/publications/focus/projecthighlights/kenyapath.htm, accessed 8 June 2003.

54 Fongkaew, W., and K. Bond. 2001. "Lifenet, Thailand: Promoting Social Action Networks for Youth Health." FOCUS Project Highlights. Washington, D.C.: FOCUS on Young Adults. Web site: www.pathfind.org/pf/pubs/focus/Project%20Highlights/lifenet5.html, accessed 6 January 2003.

55 Abaunza, H. 2002. "Sexual Health Exchange 2002-1: 'Puntos de Encuentro': Communication for Development in Nicaragua." Amsterdam: KIT Information Services, Royal Tropical Institute. Web site: www.kit.nl/ils/exchange_content/html/communication_nicaragua_-_sexu.asp, accessed 15 July 2003.

56 "Nicaraguan Youth Begin to Play It Safe." 2001. *Communication Impact!* No. 12. Baltimore, Maryland: Center for Communication Programs, Johns Hopkins University.

57 Excerpted from: Kilm, Y. M., et al. 2001. "Promoting Sexual Responsibility among Young People in Zimbabwe." *International Family Planning Perspectives* 27(1): 11-19.

58 Moch, L., and C. Stevens. 1999. "Reaching Adolescents Through Hotlines and Radio Call-In Programs." In Focus Series. FOCUS on Young Adults. Pathfinder International; "Key Youth Programs: Use Hotlines" n.d. Baltimore, Maryland: Center for Communication Programs, Johns Hopkins University. Web site: www.jhuccp.org/resources/youth/key5.html, accessed January 7, 2003; and International Planned Parenthood Federation. 2001c. "Youth Telephone Hotlines In Guatemala and Columbia." *IPPF/WHR Spotlight on Youth*. No. 5. New York: International Planned Parenthood Federation.

59 Moch and Stevens 1999.

60 Palmer, A. 2002. "Reaching Youth Worldwide." Working Paper 6. Baltimore, Maryland: Center for Communication Programs, Johns Hopkins University.

61 Ibid.

62 "Studio 263 Key in Anti-Aids Drive: Director." 5 December 2002. *The Daily News* (Harare). See Web site: allAfrica.com.

63 Family Health International. 2002. *Behavioral Surveillance Survey 1999-2000*. Arlington, Virginia: Family Health International; and Hope Enterprises Ltd. 2002a. *Report of Adolescent Condom Survey, Jamaica, 2001*. Prepared for the Commercial Market Strategies Project. Kingston, Jamaica: Hope Enterprises Ltd. Cited in: *Adolescent Reproductive Health Behaviors and Outcomes in Jamaica*, by K. Hardee, and L. Dougherty. 2002. Kingston, Jamaica: Youth.now, The Futures Group.

64 Rebourças 2002.

65 Holgate, Michael. 2000. "Programs for Adolescents: The 'Ashe' Experience in Jamaica." Network 20(3): 28-29.

66 International Planned Parenthood Federation. 2001d. *Youth and Technology: IPPF/WHR Experiences to Promote Sexual and Reproductive Health*. New York: International Planned Parenthood Federation.

67 Ibid.

68 Msimang, S., and S. Wilson (eds). 2002. *Act Now: A Resource Guide for Young Women on HIV/AIDS*. New York and Toronto: UNIFEM and Association for Women's Rights in Development. Web site: www.awid.org/publications/publications.html, accessed 5 December 2002.

69 Web site: www.bbc.co.uk/worldservice/sci_tech/features/health/sexwise, accessed 5 December 2002.

70 National Commission for International Cooperation and Sustainable Development. "The International Education Project: HIV/Aids and Youth: Beyond My Own Backyard." Amsterdam: National Commission for International Cooperation and Sustainable Development. Web site: www.ict-edu.nl/content/nederlands/learn/middenframe_aids.html, accessed 15 December 2002.

71 Web site: www.youthshakers.org.

72 Palmer 2002.

CHAPTER 5

1 UNICEF. 1998. *The Progress of Nations 1998*. New York: UNICEF; and UNICEF. 2001. *Early Marriage: Child Spouses*. Innocenti Digest. No. 7. Florence, Italy: UNICEF Innocenti Research Centre. Web site: www.unicef-icdc.org/publications/pdf/digest7e.pdf.

2 United Nations. 2001. *We the Children: End-decade Review of the Follow-up to the World Summit for Children: Report of the Secretary General (A/S-27/3)*. New York: United Nations.

3 Gaym, A. 2000. "A Review of Maternal Mortality at Jimma Hospital, Southwestern Ethiopia." *Ethiopian Journal of Health Development* 14(2): 215-223.

4 UNICEF 2001.

5 WHO. 1989. *The Reproductive Health of Adolescents: A Strategy for Action*. A Joint WHO/UNFPA/UNICEF Statement. Geneva: WHO.

6 ORC Macro. 2001. *Final Report: Bangladesh*. Calverton, Maryland: ORC Macro. Web site: www.measuredhs.com, accessed 7 July 2003.

7 Alan Guttmacher Institute. 1998. *Into a New World: Young Women's Sexual and Reproductive Lives*. New York: Alan Guttmacher Institute.

8 United Nations. 2002. *World Population Monitoring 2002: Reproductive Rights and Reproductive Health: Selected Aspects (ESA/P/WP.717)*. New York:

Commission on Population and Development, United Nations.

9 Ibid.

10 WHO. 1997. *Abortion: A Tabulation of Available Data on the Frequency and Mortality of Unsafe Abortion*, Third Edition. Geneva: WHO.

11 UNESCO. 2002. "Unwanted Pregnancy and Unsafe Abortion." *Package of Laws and Legislations Series 3: Legislation Review 2*. Bangkok: Regional Clearing House on Population, Education and Communication (RECHPEC), UNESCO.

12 Harrison, K. A. 1985. "Childbearing, Health and Social Priorities: A Survey of 22,744 Consecutive Deliveries in Zaria, Northern Nigeria." *British Journal of Obstetrics and Gynaecology* 92(Supp. 5): 1-119.

13 The definitions also use various technical rules for assigning the status of currently pregnant or amenorrheic women (e.g., using their statements about whether and when they wanted their pregnancy) and for women who do not believe they are fecund. The details of the various definitions and a discussion of their reliability and validity can be reviewed in: Casterline, J. B., and S. W. Sinding. 2000. "Unmet Need for Family Planning in Developing Countries and Policy Implications." *Population and Development Review* 26(4): 691–723; and Westoff, C. F., and A. Bankole. 1995. *Unmet Need: 1990–1994*. Demographic and Health Surveys Comparative Studies. No. 16. Calverton, Maryland: Macro International, Inc.

14 Data are from the STATcompiler on the main survey web site (www.measuredhs.com), accessed 6 May 2003. Additional surveys are being processed or are in the field and will be available prior to publication of this report.

15 Data were available for seven countries in Latin America and 23 in sub-Saharan Africa.

16 However, data were available for only three Central Asian countries.

17 Gabon, South Africa, Togo and Zimbabwe show such high levels.

18 Yemen, with four times higher unmet than met spacing needs, was the only country with less than half—only 22 per cent—of demand met.

19 Senderowitz, J. 1999. *Making Reproductive Health Services Youth Friendly*. Research, Program and Policy Series. Washington, D.C.: FOCUS on Young Adults, Pathfinder International.

20 Boland, R. 2003. Population and Law database (Harvard University). Special compendium provided on request, p. 1.

21 Ibid., pp. 1-2.

22 Family Care International. 1999. Meeting the Cairo Challenge: A Summary Report: Implementing the ICPD Programme of Action, p. 9. New York: Family Care International.

23 Boland 2003, p. 2.

24 Ibid., p. 3.

25 Ibid., pp. 1-2.

26 Senderowitz, J. 1997. *Reproductive Health Outreach Programs for Young Adults*. Pathfinder International/FOCUS on Young Adults Research Series. Washington, D.C.: FOCUS on Young Adults, Pathfinder International.

27 Erulkar, A., and B. Mensch. 1997. *Youth Centres in Kenya: Evaluation of the Family Planning Association of Kenya Programme*. Nairobi: The Population Council; The Population Council. 2000. *Overview of Youth Centre Assessments In Kenya, Zimbabwe and Ghana*. New York: The Population Council; Glover, E. K., et al. 1998. *Youth Centres in Ghana: Assessment of the Planned Parenthood Association of Ghana Programme*. Nairobi: The Population Council; and Phiri, A., and A. Erulkar. 1997. *A Situation Analysis of the Zimbabwe National Family Planning Council's Youth Centres: Baseline Assessment*. Naibori: Zimbabwe National Family Planning Council and the Population Council.

28 Action Health Incorporated. 1998. "The Youth Clinic." *Growing Up* 6(2).

29 Boucard, G. 1998. "Mid-Term Evaluation: FOSREF Reproductive Health for Adolescents Project." Prepared for UNFPA. New York: UNFPA.

30 Family Care International 1999, p. 101.

31 Ibid., p. 102.

32 Ibid., p. 99.

33 International Planned Parenthood Federation. n.d. "Burkina Faso Programme Review." Unpublished report. London: International Planned Parenthood Federation.

34 International Planned Parenthood Federation. 2001. "Integrating Sexual and Reproductive Health Services for Youth in Colombia." *IPPF/WHR Spotlight on Youth*. No. 1. New York: International Planned Parenthood Federation.

35 Russian Federation. 2002. "Information Letter on improving the activities of youth centers for protection of reproductive health of adolescents, based on the results of the UNFPA project 'Reproductive Health and Rights of People in the Russian Federation' implemented in Moscow, Tver, Saint-Petersburg, Novosibirsk, Barnaul, Tomsk in 2000-2002." Moscow: Ministry of Health, Russian Federation.

36 Jamaica Adolescent Reproductive Health Activity. November 2002. "Background Report, Mid-Term External Evaluation." Washington, D.C.: The Futures Group International in collaboration with the Ministry of Health, Margaret Sanger Center International, and Dunlop Corbin Communication.

37 Senderowitz, J., and C. Stevens. 2001. *Leveraging the For-Profit Sector in Support of Adolescent and Young Adult Reproductive Health Programming*. Washington, D.C.: Futures Institute for Sustainable Development.

38 Hughes, J. November 2000. Personal communication; and Erulkar, A. 2000. Unpublished memo.

39 Family Planning Service Expansion and Technical Support Project. 1999. "Evaluating the Impact of ZNA/MAPS Interventions on Reproductive Health Services for Youth." Lusaka, Zambia: Family Planning Service Expansion and Technical Support Project, John Snow International; and Williams, T. 14 March 2001. Personal correspondence.

40 Murray, N., et al. 2001. *Will Youth Be Negatively Affected by User Fees for Reproductive Health Products or Services?* Washington, D.C.: FOCUS on Young Adults, Pathfinder International.

CHAPTER 6

1 UNFPA organized a meeting in May 2002 in collaboration with the Population Council to review lessons learned from the first generation and discuss new approaches to programme planning, design, and evaluation and expanding efforts to address neglected subgroups of adolescents (e.g., the young married, rural and marginalized populations, etc.).

2 UNFPA. 2002. "African Youth Alliance (AYA) Programme Profile." New York: UNFPA.

3 Ibid.

4 See the EC/UNFPA Initiative for Reproductive Health (RHI) in Asia web site: www.asia-initiative.org/rhi_in_brief.html, accessed 24 February 2003.

5 Ibid.

6 Nguyen, T. H., and E. Kelly. June 2002. *Final Report. End of Project Evaluation. Adolescent Reproductive Health Service Delivery Project*. Melbourne, Australia: Marie Stopes International. Vietnam.

7 Nguyen T. G. 22 January 2003. "The Youth House." Presentation to the Orientation Workshop for RHPs [Reproductive Health Projects] Partners, Pathfinder International/Viet Nam, Hanoi, Viet Nam, 22 January 2003.

8 Hainsworth, G. 2002. *Providing Reproductive Health and STI/HIV Information and Services to This Generation: Insights from the Geração Biz Experience*. Watertown, Massachusetts: Pathfinder International.

9 Ibid.

10 Ibid.

11 Senderowitz, J. July 2002. Field observations and meetings.

12 The Population Council. 1998. *What Can Be Done to Foster Multisectoral Population Policies: Summary Report of a Seminar*, Overseas Development Council, Washington, D.C., 28 May 1997. Washington, D.C.: The Population Council.

CHAPTER 7

1 Research methodologies are increasingly including measures of the personal characteristics of adolescents, their family situations and community characteristics and norms.

2 The United Nations Theme Group on HIV/AIDS in China. 2002. *HIV/AIDS: China's Titanic Peril. 2001 Update of the AIDS Situation and Needs Assessment Report*. Beijing, China: UNAIDS.

3 Monitoring the AIDS Pandemic (MAP) Network. 2001. "The Status and Trends of HIV/AIDS/STI Epidemics in Asia and the Pacific". Report presented at the MAP Meeting in Melbourne, Australia, 4 October 2001.

4 Rosen, J. 2001. *Formulating and Implementing National Youth Policy: Lessons from Bolivia and the Dominican Republic*. Washington, D.C.: FOCUS on Young Adults, Pathfinder International.

5 Greene, M., et al. 2002. *In this Generation: Sexual & Reproductive Health Policies for a Youthful World*. Washington, D.C.: Population Action International.

6 Ministry of Health. 2002. *National Standards and Guidelines for Reproductive Health Care Services*. Hanoi: Ministry of Health, Government of Viet Nam.

7 UNFPA. 1999. *Annual Report 1999*. New York: UNFPA.

8 Kiragu, K., et al. 1998. *Adolescent Reproductive Health Needs in Kenya: A Communication Response Evaluation of The Kenya Initiatives Project*. Baltimore, Maryland: Population Communication Services, John Hopkins University.

9 United Nations. 1989. *Convention on the Rights of the Child: General Assembly Resolution 25(XLIV): 44th Session: Supplement No. 49, (A/RES/44/25, reprinted in 28 I.L.M. 1448): opened for signature 26 January 1990*, paragraph 29.1(b); United Nations. 1979. *Convention on the Elimination of All Forms of Discrimination against Women: Adopted and Opened for Signature, Ratification and Accession by General Assembly Resolution 34/180 of 18 December 1979*, article 10c. New York: United Nations; United Nations. 1993. *Vienna Declaration and Programme of Action: World Conference on Human Rights (A/CONF.157/24)*, paragraph 18. New York: United Nations; United Nations. 1995. *Population and Development*, vol. 1: *Programme of Action adopted at the International Conference on Population and Development: Cairo, 5-13 September 1994*, Principle 10, paragraphs 4.3(c), 4.12, 4.16(a, b), 4.17, 4.29, 7.39, 7.48 and 11.16. New York: Department of Economic and Social Information and Policy Analysis, United Nations; United Nations. 1996. *The Beijing Declaration and the Platform for Action: Fourth World Conference on Women: Beijing, China: 4-15 September 1995* (DPI/1766/Wom), paragraphs 83(i), 107(e), 125(e), 126(b), 227, 230(f), 231c, 233(c, d, f, g) and 278(b, c). New York: Department of Public Information, United Nations; United Nations. 1999. *Key Actions for the Further Implementation of the Programme of Action of the International Conference on Population and Development (A/S-21/5/Add.1)*, paragraphs 3 and 40. New York: United Nations; and United Nations. 2000. *Resolution Adopted by the General Assembly: S-23/3: Further Actions and Initiatives to Implement the Beijing Declaration and Platform for Action*

(A/RES/S-23/3), paragraph 99(a). New York: United Nations.

10 United Nations 1995, paragraphs 7.38, 12.13, 12.14, 12.20, 12.22; United Nations 1996, paragraphs 109(d, and f), 206(a, b, i, and j), and 231e; and United Nations 1999, paragraphs 5, 37.

11 United Nations 1989, paragraph 3.1; United Nations 1995, paragraphs 6.7(b) and 7.21; United Nations 1996, paragraphs 107(e), 110(a, and e),111(a), and 267; United Nations 1999, paragraphs 21(b), 40, 42, 45, 52(b), and 73(c); and United Nations 2000, paragraphs 72(g), and 79(f).

12 United Nations 1979, paragraphs 7(c), and 14.2(a); United Nations 1995, paragraphs 4.3(b), 4.4(a), 7.9, 7.18, 15.8, 15.9, and 15.10; United Nations 1996, paragraphs 106(s), 108(a, and j), 233(f), and 295; and United Nations 2000, paragraphs 51, 52(c), 76, and 81.

13 United Nations 1989, paragraphs 12.1, and 13; United Nations 1995, paragraphs 6.15, 7.43, 7.47, and 11.20; United Nations 1996, paragraphs 111(b), and 284(a, and b); United Nations 1999, paragraphs 21(b), 73(c), 83, and 90; United Nations 2000, paragraphs 79(f), and 95(b, and c).

14 Senderowitz, J. 2000. "A Review of Program Approaches to Adolescent Reproductive Health." Poptech Assignment. No. 2000.176. Arlington, Virginia: Population Technical Assistance Project.

15 Chibbamulilo, P. 1997. *A Report on the Mini-Participatory Learning and Action (PLA) Exercise for the JSI/SEATS Programme in Zambia.* Lusaka, Zambia: Family Planning Service Expansion and Technical Support Project, John Snow International.

16 MacLean, A. 1999. *Sewing a Better Future: A Report of Discussions with Young Garment Factory Workers about Life, Work and Sexual Health.* Washington, D.C.: CARE International, Cambodia, and FOCUS on Young Adults.

17 Cheetham, N., R. Thiombiano, and S. Ky. 2003. "Community Participation to Improve Youth Sexual and Reproductive Health in Burkina Faso." Unpublished project summary. Washington, D.C.: Advocates for Youth.

18 Khan, S. A., and M. Ahmed. 2001. "BRAC, Bangladesh: Community Mobilization to Support Adolescent Development." FOCUS Project Highlights. Washington, D.C.: FOCUS on Young Adults, Pathfinder International. Web site: www.pathfind.org/pf/pubs/focus/Project%20Highlights/ BRAC.htm, accessed 6 January 2003.

19 Micklewright, J. 2002. "Social Exclusion and Children: A European View for a US Debate." Innocenti Working Papers. No. 90. Florence, Italy: Innocenti Research Centre, UNICEF.

20 Lansdown, G. 2001. *Promoting Children's Participation in Democratic Decision-Making.* UNICEF Insight No. 6. Florence, Italy: Innocenti Research Center, UNICEF. Web site: www.unicef-icdc.org/publications/pdf/insight6.pdf, accessed 19 April 2003.

21 Cornwall, A., and A. Welbourn (eds.). 2002. *Realizing Rights: Transforming Approaches to Sexual and Reproductive Well-being.* London: Zed Books.

22 See: UNICEF. 2002. *The State of the World's Children 2002: Leadership* (Sales No. E.02.XX.1). New York: UNICEF.

23 Faulkner, K., and J. Knott. 2002. "Institutionalising Youth Participation in a Large International Organisation: Experiences from the International Planned Parenthood Federation." Ch. 2 in Cornwall and Welbourn 2002.

24 Lansdown 2001.

25 Ibid.

26 See: UNESCO. n.d. "Who is Who: Directory of International Youth-led/Youth-serving Organisations." Paris: UNESCO. Web site: www.unesco.org/youth/ONGRepertoire.htm, accessed 8 June 2003.

27 Russell, J., and X. Solórzano. 2001. *Adolescent and Youth Policy: The Experiences of Colombia, Dominican Republic and Nicaragua.* Washington, D.C.: Adolescent Health and Development, PAHO, WHO.

28 See web site: www.elige.org.mx/Quienes_somos.htm, accessed 20 January 2003.

29 TakingItGlobal Projects: Network of Young Women Activists against Violence against Women. See web site: http://projects.takingitglobal.org/genderviolence, accessed 20 January 2003.

30 The Youth Coalition, Ottawa, Ontario, Canada. Web site: www.youthcoalition.org, accessed 20 January 2003.

31 For example, the costs of an HIV/AIDS preventive education programme in a country with low prevalence may be high relative to the immediate benefits. However, the risk of spread in an uninformed population is greatly increased with enormous potential consequences.

32 Costs are not the same as expenditures. Administrative costs, private costs and opportunity costs are often omitted from analyses. Modes of financing (e.g., transfers) are variously, and often improperly, accounted. See: Knowles, J., and J. Behrman. 2003. Background paper (edited version March 2003) for the Expert Meeting on Assessing the Economic Benefit of Investing in Youth in Developing Countries, National Research Council, Washington, D.C., 15 October 2003.

33 Correia, M., and W. Cunningham, W. 2003. *Caribbean Youth Development: Issues and Policy Directions.* Washington, D.C.: The World Bank; and Cunningham, W. 2003. Presentation at the Expert Meeting on Assessing the Economic Benefit of Investing in Youth in Developing Countries, National Research Council, Washington, D.C., 15 October 2003.

34 It is easier to estimate social than private costs as the latter component inputs and their prices vary.

35 The financial costs include child support payments, the publicly paid health costs for the mother and child, government transfers for aid to poor families and to foster care. Economic costs include tax revenues foregone by lowered future income of the mother and the child, administrative resources diverted to providing social services, lost benefits from alternative uses of health care funds, economic costs of increases in crime related to reduced education and employment prospects and other reduced contributions to society by the child and adolescent mother. For additional references and details, see: Correia and Cunningham 2003; and Cunningham 2003. Variations in social services provided and income levels (and the portion directed to child support) account for the differences in national estimates.

36 Buvinic, M. 1998. "The Costs of Adolescent Childbearing: Evidence from Chile, Barbados, Guatemala and Mexico." *Studies in Family Planning* 29(2): 201-209.

37 The biological father is less likely to be present and more of the women are living as boarders outside their own or their parents' home. Unlike in the United States (see: Buvinic 1998 for references), future marital chances are not affected. The pattern of extended single-motherhood for young mothers does not hold in these Latin American settings.

38 In Mexico, two thirds of adolescent mothers were children of women who were themselves adolescent mothers.

39 Population-based surveys would be the most reliable, though costly, method. Most information comes from measures at antenatal centres but young mothers may be less likely to use them.

40 Cited in: Knowles and Behrman 2003, p. 41. This estimate contains a significant time discount for a gain of 34.6 disability-adjusted life years that are realized 5-8 years after infection.

41 Marseille, E., P. B. Hoffman, and J. G. Kahn. 2002. "HIV Prevention before HAART in Sub-Saharan Africa." *The Lancet.* 2002 359(9320): 1851-1856.

42 This point was forcefully argued by P. Piot, D. Zewdie, and T. Türmen (2003. "HIV/AIDS Prevention and Treatment." *The Lancet* 360[9326]: 86) in their rejoinder to the Marseille, Hoffman and Khan 2002 article.

43 Benefits included saved disability adjusted life years, reductions in secondary infections of partners of the averted case and reduced annual medical care costs.

44 Marek, T., and J.M. Del Rosso, T. 1996. *Class Action: Improving School Performance in the Developing World through Better Health and Nutrition.* Washington, D.C.: The World Bank. Cited in: Knowles and Behrman 2003.

45 WHO. 1996. "Research to Improve Implementation and Effectiveness of School Health Programmes," (WHO/HPR/HEP/96.3). Geneva: WHO. Cited in: Knowles and Behrman 2003. The reviews show high returns (in the area of 18-20:1) to anti-smoking interventions, consistent with the high rates of prevalence and associated long-term mortality and morbidity.

46 This is the upper range of estimates for needs to meet the education-related Millennium Development Goals and is based on applying normative investment standards related to national GNP. A range of estimates from $2.4 billion, including UNICEF's estimate of $9.1 billion, is noted. See: Devarajan, S. 2002. "External Finance and the Millennium Development Goals." Presentation at the International Seminar, "Latin America and the Caribbean: Challenges before the Millennium Development Goals," organized by the Inter-American Development Bank, Economic Commission for Latin America and the Caribbean, the World Bank, and UNDP, Washington, D.C., 10-11 June 2002.

47 The plausible range of estimates of returns, depending on assumptions about annual discount rates and component returns, was from 2.77 to 25.63 times the costs. See: Knowles and Behrman 2003, Ch. 6.

48 The uncertainty in this estimate was considerably higher; the range was 8.14 to 1,764.

Sources for Boxes

CHAPTER 1

2 United Nations. 1999. *Key Actions for the Further Implementation of the Programme of Action of the International Conference on Population and Development* (A/S-21/5/Add.1), paragraph 73. New York: United Nations; United Nations Committee on the Rights of the Child. 2003. "General Comment No. 4 (2003): Adolescent Health and Development in the Context of the Convention on the Rights of the Child" (CRC/GC/2003/4), 33rd session, paragraph 21. New York: United Nations; and United Nations. 1999. "General Recommendation 24: Article of the Convention on the Elimination of All Forms of Discrimination against Women: Women and Health Article 12," paragraph 8. *Report of the Committee on the Elimination of Discrimination against Women: Twentieth Session* (A/54/38 [Part 1]). New York: United Nations.

3 United Nations. 2003. *World Population Prospects: The 2002 Revision.* New York: Population Division, Department of Economic and Social Affairs.

4 See web site: www.swcp.com/shinealight/Pages/Caracol.html, accessed 20 December 2002; and the Child Welfare Scheme. 2002. Web site: www.childwelfarescheme.org, accessed 20 December 2002.

5 Women's Commission for Refugee Women and Children. 2002. "Precious Resources: Participatory Research Study with Adolescents and Youth in Sierra Leone: April-July 2002." New York: Women's Commission for Refugee Women and Children. Web site: www.womenscommission.org/reports/sl/01.html, accessed 30 June 2003.

6 Cook, R., and B. M. Dickens. 2000. "Recognizing Adolescents' 'Evolving Capacities' to Exercise Choice in Reproductive Health Care," p. 16. *International Journal of Gynecology and Obstetrics* 70(1): 13-21.

CHAPTER 2

7 Bruce, J. 2002. "Married Adolescent Girls: Human Rights, Health and Developmental Needs of a Neglected Majority." United Nations Special Session on Children, New York, 8-10 May 2002.

8 UNFPA. 2003. "Afghan Teens Speak Out Against Early Marriage: World Population Day: A Personal Story." News feature. New York: UNFPA.

9 Barkat, A., et al. 1999. *The RSDP/Pathfinder Bangladesh Newlywed Strategy: Results of an Assessment.* Washington, D.C.: FOCUS on Young Adults; and Bond, K., and L. MacLaren. 1998. "Report on Consultancy to NIPHP Partners, Bangladesh, 19 November-14 December 1998." Washington, D.C.: FOCUS on Young Adults.

10 Campbell, C., and C. MacPhail. 2002. "Peer Education, Gender and the Development of Critical Consciousness: Participatory HIV Prevention by South African Youth," p. 332. *Social Science and Medicine* 55(2): 331-345; Brown, A., et al. 2001. *Sexual Relations among Young People in Developing Countries: Evidence from WHO Case Studies* (WHO/RHR/01.8). Occasional Paper. Geneva: Family and Community Health, Department of Reproductive Health and Research, and WHO; Eggleston, E., J. Jackson, and K. Hardee. 1999. "Sexual Attitudes and Behaviour among Young Adolescents in Jamaica." *International Family Planning Perspectives* 25(2): 78-85; and Barker, G. 2000. "Gender-Equitable Boys in a Gender Inequitable World: Reflections From Qualitative Research and Programme Development in Rio de Janeiro." *Sexual and Relationship Therapy* 15(3): 262-282.

CHAPTER 3

11 Shelton, J. 29 July 2002. "ABC Approach to Behaviour Change." Jim Shelton's Pearls. Web site: www.jhuccp.org/pearls/2002/07-29.shtml.

12 Population Services International and Population Reference Bureau. 2000. *Social Marketing for Adolescent Sexual Health: Results of Operations Research Projects in Botswana, Cameroon, Guinea, and South Africa.* Washington, D.C.: Population Services International and Population Reference Bureau.

13 Horizons Program, Kenya Project Partners, and Uganda Project Partners. 2001. *HIV Voluntary Counseling and Testing Among Youth: Results from an Exploratory Study in Nairobi, Kenya, and Kampala and Masaka, Uganda.* Washington, D.C.: Horizons Program, the Population Council.

CHAPTER 4

14 Hogle, J. A., et al. 2002. "What Happened in Uganda: Declining HIV Prevalence, Behaviour Change and the National Response." *Project Lessons Learned Case Study.* September. Washington, D.C.: USAID; and Wendo, C. 2002. "School HIV/AIDS Manual Ready." Kampala, Uganda: New Vision. Web site: www.allAfrica.com, accessed 5 December 2002.

15 Stewart, H., et al. 2001. *Reducing HIV Infection Among Youth: What Can Schools Do: Key Baseline Findings from Mexico, South Africa, and Thailand.* Washington, D.C.: Horizons Program, the Population Council.

16 Ryan, W. A. September 2002. Interview with Mmagokgoshi Morema.

17 Rose-Avila, M. 1990. "Peer Education with Gang Members: Protecting Life and Health." FOCUS Project Highlights. Washington, D.C.: FOCUS on Young Adults. Web site: www.pathfind.org/pf/pubs/focus/Project%20Highlights/homies.html, accessed 6 January 2003.

18 UNFPA. 5 June 2003. "Moving Beyond Excuses: Eastern European Ad Campaign Promotes Condom Use." News feature. New York: UNFPA. Web site: www.unfpa.org/news/news.cfm?ID=326.

CHAPTER 5

20 Murray C., and A. Lopez. 1998. Health Dimensions of Sex and Reproduction: The Global Burden of Sexually Transmitted Diseases, HIV, Maternal Conditions, Perinatal Disorders and Congenital Anomalies. Geneva: WHO; and UNFPA and EngenderHealth. 2003. Obstetric Fistula Needs Assessment Report: Findings from Nine African Countries. New York: UNFPA and EngenderHealth.

21 Senderowitz, J. 1999. *Making Reproductive Health Services Youth Friendly.* Research, Program and Policy Series. Washington, D.C.: FOCUS on Young Adults, Pathfinder International.

22 Barkat, A., et al. 1999. *The RSDP/Pathfinder Bangladesh Newlywed Strategy: Results of an Assessment.* Washington, D.C.: FOCUS on Young Adults; and Bond, K., and L. MacLaren. 1998. "Report on Consultancy to NIPHP Partners, Bangladesh, 19 November-14 December 1998." Washington, D.C.: FOCUS on Young Adults.

CHAPTER 6

23 Dickson-Tetteh, K., A. Pettifor, and W. Moleko. 2001. "Working with Public Sector Clinics to Provide Adolescent-Friendly Services in South Africa." *Reproductive Health Matters* 9(17): 160-169. See also: Kaiser Family Foundation web site: www.kff.org/docs/sections/safrica/loveLife.html.

24 UNFPA. 2003. "Project RLA/97/P07: The Right to Have Dreams and a Duty to Plan Them." Project report submitted by UNFPA Panama Field Office.

25 Bernstein, S. November 2002. Site visit.

CHAPTER 7

26 United Nations. 2000. *Resolution Adopted by the General Assembly: 55/2: United Nations Millennium Declaration* (A/RES/55/2). New York: United Nations. See also web site: www.un.org/millenniumgoals.

27 Rosen, J. 2001. *Formulating and Implementing National Youth Policy: Lessons from Bolivia and the Dominican Republic.* Washington, D.C.: FOCUS on Young Adults, Pathfinder International.

28 Material submitted by: Bogaarts, Y. 2003. World Population Foundation.

29 Barcelona, D., Adolescent Youth Cluster, UNFPA. 2003. Personal communication.

30 UNFPA. 18 March 2002. News Feature. Web site: www.unfpa.org/news/news.cfm?ID=116&Language=1.

32 United Nations. 1999. *Key Actions for the Further Implementation of the Programme of Action of the International Conference on Population and Development* (A/S-21/5 Add. 1). New York: United Nations.

	Indicators of Mortality			Indicators of Education				Reproductive Health Indicators			
	Infant mortality Total per 1,000 live births	Life expectancy M/F	Maternal mortality ratio	Primary enrolment (gross) M/F	Proportion reaching grade 5 M/F	Secondary enrolment (gross) M/F	% Illiterate (>15 years) M/F	Births per 1,000 women aged 15-19	Contraceptive Prevalence Any method	Modern methods	HIV prevalence rate (%) (15-24) M/F
World Total	56	63.3 / 67.6	386					50	61	54	
More developed regions (*)	8	72.1 / 79.4						27	69	56	
Less developed regions (+)	61	61.7 / 65.1						53	59	54	
Least developed countries (‡)	97	48.8 / 50.5						124			
AFRICA (1)	89	47.9 / 50.0						107	25	20	
EASTERN AFRICA	97	42.4 / 43.8						117	21	16	
Burundi	107	40.4 / 41.4	866	73 / 58	59 / 58	12 / 9	44 / 60	50	9	1	4.95 / 11.05
Eritrea	73	51.2 / 54.2	857	65 / 54	69 / 69	34 / 23	33 / 55	115	5	4	2.75 / 4.30
Ethiopia	100	44.6 / 46.3	1,193	76 / 52	64 / 64	22 / 14	53 / 69	100	8	6	4.40 / 7.80
Kenya	69	43.5 / 45.6	1,564	95 / 93	70 / 73	32 / 29	11 / 24	78	39	32	6.00 / 15.55
Madagascar	91	52.5 / 54.8	654	105 / 101	45 / 48	15 / 14	26 / 40	137	19	12	0.07 / 0.24
Malawi	115	37.3 / 37.7	1,936	139 / 135	55 / 43	40 / 31	26 / 53	163	31	26	6.35 / 14.90
Mauritius (2)	16	68.4 / 75.8	32	109 / 108		79 / 75	12 / 19	33	75	49	
Mozambique	122	36.6 / 39.6	936	104 / 79	62 / 54	14 / 9	40 / 71	105	6	5	6.10 / 14.70
Rwanda	112	38.8 / 39.7	1,258	119 / 118	38 / 40	12 / 12	26 / 40	50	13	4	4.90 / 11.20
Somalia	118	46.4 / 49.5	685					213			
Uganda	86	45.4 / 46.9	910	143 / 129		21 / 16	23 / 43	211	23	18	2.00 / 4.65
United Republic of Tanzania	100	42.5 / 44.1	1,408	63 / 63	80 / 83	6 / 5	16 / 33	120	25	17	3.55 / 8.05
Zambia	105	32.7 / 32.1	770	80 / 76	83 / 78	26 / 21	15 / 28	145	25	14	8.10 / 21.00
Zimbabwe	58	33.7 / 32.6	654	96 / 93		47 / 42	7 / 15	92	54	50	12.40 / 33.00
MIDDLE AFRICA (3)	116	41.6 / 43.8						200	10	3	
Angola	140	38.8 / 41.5	820	78 / 69		18 / 13		229	8	4	2.20 / 5.70
Cameroon	88	45.1 / 47.4	748	115 / 100	72 / 93	22 / 17	21 / 36	121	19	7	5.40 / 12.65
Central African Republic	100	38.5 / 40.6	834	89 / 61			40 / 65	132	15	3	5.85 / 13.50
Chad	115	43.7 / 45.7	933	90 / 57	58 / 48	18 / 5	48 / 66	195	8	2	2.35 / 4.30
Congo, Democratic Republic of the (4)	120	40.8 / 42.8	755	49 / 44		24 / 13	27 / 50	230	8	2	2.90 / 5.90
Congo, Republic of	84	46.6 / 49.7	406	101 / 93		46 / 38	13 / 26	146			3.25 / 7.80
Gabon	57	55.8 / 57.5	446	144 / 143		61 / 58		113	33	12	
NORTHERN AFRICA (5)	49	64.5 / 68.2						36	47	42	
Algeria	44	68.1 / 71.3	103	116 / 107	97 / 98	68 / 73	24 / 43	16	64	50	
Egypt	41	66.7 / 71.0	84	103 / 96	99 / 100	88 / 83	33 / 56	47	56	54	
Libyan Arab Jamahiriya	21	70.8 / 75.4	130	115 / 117		88 / 91	9 / 32	7	40	26	
Morocco	42	66.8 / 70.5	238	101 / 88	79 / 81	44 / 35	38 / 64	25	50	42	
Sudan	77	54.1 / 57.1	352	59 / 51	86 / 88	22 / 36	31 / 54	55	8	7	1.10 / 3.10
Tunisia	23	70.8 / 74.9	68	120 / 115	92 / 94	76 / 80	19 / 39	7	60	51	
SOUTHERN AFRICA	52	43.9 / 49.1						66	52	51	
Botswana	57	38.9 / 40.5	275	108 / 108	84 / 89	90 / 96	25 / 20	91	40	39	16.10 / 37.50
Lesotho	92	32.3 / 37.7	437	112 / 118	68 / 80	30 / 36	27 / 6	53	30	30	17.40 / 38.10
Namibia	60	42.9 / 45.6	274	112 / 113	92 / 93	58 / 65	17 / 19	78	29	26	11.10 / 24.25
South Africa	48	45.1 / 50.7	239	115 / 108	66 / 63	83 / 91	14 / 15	66	56	55	10.65 / 25.65
Swaziland	78	33.3 / 35.4	380	128 / 121	83 / 85	60 / 60	19 / 21	45	20	17	15.25 / 39.50
WESTERN AFRICA (6)	90	49.0 / 50.3						119	15	8	
Benin	93	48.4 / 53.0	767	113 / 78	89 / 78	30 / 14	48 / 76	107	19	7	1.17 / 3.75
Burkina Faso	93	45.2 / 46.2	818	52 / 37	68 / 71	12 / 8	66 / 86	136	12	5	4.00 / 9.75
Côte d'Ivoire	101	40.8 / 41.2	459	92 / 70	91 / 90	30 / 17	41 / 63	116	15	7	2.90 / 8.35
Gambia	81	52.7 / 55.5	526	86 / 78	75 / 63	43 / 30	56 / 70	125	10	9	0.53 / 1.34

	Indicators of Mortality			Indicators of Education				Reproductive Health Indicators			
	Infant mortality Total per 1,000 live births	Life expectancy M/F	Maternal mortality ratio	Primary enrolment (gross) M/F	Proportion reaching grade 5 M/F	Secondary enrolment (gross) M/F	% Illiterate (>15 years) M/F	Births per 1,000 women aged 15-19	Contraceptive Prevalence Any method	Contraceptive Prevalence Modern methods	HIV prevalence rate (%) (15-24) M/F
Ghana	58	56.5 / 59.3	407	84 / 76	67 / 65	40 / 32	20 / 37	76	22	13	1.38 / 3.00
Guinea	102	48.8 / 49.5	822	78 / 56	90 / 77	20 / 7		163	6	4	
Guinea-Bissau	120	43.8 / 46.9	1,017	99 / 66	41 / 34	26 / 14	46 / 77	197	8	4	1.05 / 2.95
Liberia	147	40.7 / 42.2	476	140 / 96	49 / 17	45 / 32	30 / 63	227	6	6	
Mali	119	48.0 / 49.1	1,135	71 / 51	100 / 86	20 / 10	64 / 84	191	8	6	1.35 / 2.10
Mauritania	97	50.9 / 54.1	889	86 / 80	68 / 55	22 / 20	49 / 70	104	8	5	
Niger	126	45.9 / 46.5	1,090	42 / 29	76 / 71	8 / 5	76 / 92	233	14	4	
Nigeria	79	51.1 / 51.8	533				28 / 44	103	15	9	3.00 / 5.85
Senegal	61	50.8 / 55.1	474	79 / 70	75 / 69	21 / 14	53 / 72	86	13	8	0.19 / 0.54
Sierra Leone	177	33.1 / 35.5	1,297	106 / 80		29 / 24		212	4	4	2.50 / 7.55
Togo	81	48.2 / 51.1	752	138 / 110	78 / 69	54 / 24	28 / 57	81	24	7	2.05 / 5.90
ASIA	**53**	**65.5 / 69.0**						**35**	**64**	**58**	
EASTERN ASIA (7)	34	69.7 / 74.7						5	82	81	
China	37	68.9 / 73.3	56	105 / 108		66 / 60	8 / 22	5	84	83	0.16 / 0.09
Democratic People's Republic of Korea	45	60.5 / 66.0	131					2	62	53	
Hong Kong SAR, China (8)	4	77.3 / 82.8					3 / 11	6	86	80	
Japan	3	77.9 / 85.1	9[9]	101 / 101		102 / 103		4	59	53	0.02 / 0.04
Mongolia	58	61.9 / 65.9	225	97 / 101		55 / 67	1 / 2	54	60	46	
Republic of Korea	5	71.8 / 79.3	20	101 / 101		94 / 94	1 / 4	3	81	67	0.03 / 0.01
SOUTH-EASTERN ASIA	41	64.4 / 69.1						42	58	49	
Cambodia	73	55.2 / 59.5	404	117 / 103	63 / 63	24 / 13	20 / 43	60	24	19	0.99 / 2.50
Indonesia	42	64.8 / 68.8	226	111 / 109	92 / 102	58 / 56	8 / 18	55	57	55	0.07 / 0.06
Lao People's Democratic Republic	88	53.3 / 55.8	622	121 / 104	58 / 60	44 / 31	24 / 47	91	32	29	0.05 / 0.03
Malaysia	10	70.8 / 75.7	41	99 / 99		67 / 74	9 / 17	18	55	30	0.70 / 0.12
Myanmar	83	54.6 / 60.2	402	89 / 89	65 / 64	40 / 38	11 / 20	24	33	28	
Philippines	29	68.0 / 72.0	213	113 / 113		74 / 81	5 / 5	38	47	28	0.02 / 0.02
Singapore	3	75.9 / 80.3	3				4 / 12	6	74	73	0.15 / 0.16
Thailand	20	65.3 / 73.5	44	97 / 93	96 / 99	84 / 80	3 / 6	49	72	70	1.09 / 1.65
Viet Nam	34	66.9 / 71.6	125	109 / 102		70 / 64	6 / 9	21	75	56	0.32 / 0.17
SOUTH CENTRAL ASIA	68	62.5 / 63.9						54	48	41	
Afghanistan	162	43.0 / 43.3	1,276	29 / 0				111	5	4	
Bangladesh	64	61.0 / 61.8	377	100 / 101	68 / 76	45 / 47	51 / 70	117	54	43	0.01 / 0.01
Bhutan	54	62.0 / 64.5	488		89 / 92			54	19	19	
India	64	63.2 / 64.6	540	111 / 92	70 / 65	57 / 40	32 / 55	45	48	43	0.34 / 0.71
Iran (Islamic Republic of)	33	68.9 / 71.9	76	88 / 85	99 / 98	81 / 75	17 / 31	33	73	56	0.05 / 0.01
Nepal	71	60.1 / 59.6	905	128 / 108	67 / 76	58 / 43	41 / 76	117	39	35	0.27 / 0.28
Pakistan	87	61.2 / 60.9	476	93 / 54		29 / 19	43 / 72	50	28	20	0.06 / 0.05
Sri Lanka	20	69.9 / 75.9	92	107 / 104		70 / 74	6 / 11	22	66	44	0.03 / 0.04
WESTERN ASIA	44	67.1 / 71.3						47	47	28	
Iraq	83	59.2 / 62.3	336	111 / 91		47 / 29	45 / 77	38	14	10	
Israel	6	77.1 / 81.0	4	114 / 114		94 / 93	3 / 7	17	68	52	
Jordan	24	69.7 / 72.5	41	101 / 101	98 / 97	86 / 89	5 / 16	27	53	38	
Kuwait	11	74.9 / 79.0	7	85 / 84		55 / 56	16 / 20	31	50	41	
Lebanon	17	71.9 / 75.1	126	101 / 97	95 / 99	72 / 79	8 / 20	25	61	37	
Occupied Palestinian Territory	21	70.8 / 74.0	57	107 / 109		80 / 86		94			
Oman	20	71.0 / 74.4	99	74 / 71	95 / 97	69 / 67	20 / 38	66	24	18	

	Indicators of Mortality			Indicators of Education				Reproductive Health Indicators			
	Infant mortality Total per 1,000 live births	Life expectancy M/F	Maternal mortality ratio	Primary enrolment (gross) M/F	Proportion reaching grade 5 M/F	Secondary enrolment (gross) M/F	% Illiterate (>15 years) M/F	Births per 1,000 women aged 15-19	Contraceptive Prevalence Any method	Modern methods	HIV prevalence rate (%) (15-24) M/F
Saudi Arabia	21	71.1 / 73.7	23	69 / 66	94 / 94	71 / 64	17 / 33	38	32	29	
Syrian Arab Republic	22	70.6 / 73.1	154	113 / 105		46 / 41	12 / 40	34	36	28	
Turkey (10)	40	68.0 / 73.2	88	105 / 96		67 / 48	7 / 24	43	64	38	
United Arab Emirates	14	73.3 / 77.4	77	99 / 99	98 / 98	71 / 80	25 / 21	51	28	24	
Yemen	71	58.9 / 61.1	488	96 / 61		69 / 25	32 / 75	111	21	10	
EUROPE	**9**	**70.1 / 78.2**						**20**	**67**	**49**	
EASTERN EUROPE	**14**	**64.0 / 74.4**						**29**	**61**	**35**	
Bulgaria	15	67.4 / 74.6	28	105 / 102		95 / 93	1 / 2	41	42	25	
Czech Republic	6	72.1 / 78.7	9	105 / 104	101 / 100	93 / 96		17	72	63	
Hungary	9	67.7 / 76.0	10	103 / 101		98 / 99	1 / 1	21	77	68	0.10 / 0.02
Poland	9	69.8 / 78.0	9	100 / 99	99 / 99	103 / 100	0 / 0	16	49	19	0.09 / 0.05
Romania	20	67.0 / 74.2	58	100 / 98		82 / 83	1 / 3	37	64	30	
Slovakia	8	69.8 / 77.6	11	103 / 103		87 / 88		24	74	41	
NORTHERN EUROPE (11)	**5**	**74.9 / 80.5**						**17**	**78**	**75**	
Denmark	5	74.2 / 79.1	8	102 / 102		125 / 131		7	78	72	0.14 / 0.07
Estonia	9	66.5 / 76.8	39	105 / 101	100 / 99	91 / 92	0 / 0	26	70	56	2.50 / 0.62
Finland	4	74.4 / 81.5	5	102 / 101	99 / 101	120 / 133		8	77	75	0.04 / 0.03
Ireland	6	74.4 / 79.6	24	120 / 119	98 / 99			15			0.06 / 0.05
Latvia	14	65.6 / 76.2	55	101 / 100		90 / 92	0 / 0	24	48	39	0.93 / 0.24
Lithuania	9	67.5 / 77.6	19	102 / 101		96 / 95	0 / 1	26	47	31	0.16 / 0.05
Norway	5	76.0 / 81.9	14	101 / 102		113 / 116		11	74	69	0.08 / 0.04
Sweden	3	77.6 / 82.6	4	109 / 111		132 / 166		7	78	72	0.07 / 0.05
United Kingdom	5	75.7 / 80.7	10	99 / 99		144 / 169		20	82	82	0.10 / 0.05
SOUTHERN EUROPE (12)	**7**	**74.6 / 81.0**						**11**	**68**	**48**	
Albania	25	70.9 / 76.7	73	107 / 107		77 / 80	8 / 23	16	58	15	
Bosnia & Herzegovina	14	71.3 / 76.7	29					23	48	16	
Croatia	8	70.3 / 78.1	12				1 / 3	19			
Greece	6	75.7 / 80.9	8	99 / 99		98 / 99	2 / 4	10			0.14 / 0.07
Italy	5	75.5 / 81.9	10	101 / 100	99 / 98	97 / 95	1 / 2	6	60	39	0.29 / 0.26
Macedonia (Former Yugoslav Republic of)	16	71.4 / 75.8	12	99 / 99		85 / 83		34			
Portugal	6	72.6 / 79.6	9	122 / 120		111 / 117	5 / 10	17	66	33	0.41 / 0.19
Serbia and Montenegro	13	70.9 / 75.6	14					26	58	33	
Slovenia	6	72.6 / 79.8	11	101 / 100			0 / 0	8	74	59	
Spain	5	75.9 / 82.8	20	105 / 105		113 / 119	1 / 3	6	81	67	0.52 / 0.24
WESTERN EUROPE (13)	**5**	**75.3 / 81.7**						**10**	**74**	**71**	
Austria	5	75.4 / 81.5	4	104 / 103		101 / 97		12	51	47	0.23 / 0.12
Belgium	4	75.7 / 81.9	10	105 / 104				9	78	74	0.12 / 0.12
France	5	75.2 / 82.8	22	106 / 104	98 / 99	107 / 108		9	75	69	0.26 / 0.18
Germany	5	75.2 / 81.2	11	104 / 104		100 / 99		11	75	72	0.10 / 0.05
Netherlands	5	75.6 / 81.0	10	109 / 106		126 / 122		5	79	76	0.20 / 0.09
Switzerland	5	75.9 / 82.3	6	108 / 107	101 / 101	103 / 96		5	82	78	0.46 / 0.40
LATIN AMERICA & CARIBBEAN	**32**	**67.1 / 73.9**						**72**	**69**	**60**	
CARIBBEAN (14)	**35**	**64.9 / 69.0**						**71**	**59**	**56**	
Cuba	7	74.8 / 78.7	33	104 / 100	95 / 96	83 / 87	3 / 3	65	70	67	0.09 / 0.05
Dominican Republic	36	64.4 / 69.2	150	126 / 122	71 / 79	53 / 67	16 / 16	93	64	59	2.10 / 2.75
Haiti	63	49.0 / 50.0	661			48 / 52		64	27	21	4.05 / 4.95

	Indicators of Mortality			Indicators of Education				Reproductive Health Indicators			
	Infant mortality Total per 1,000 live births	Life expectancy M/F	Maternal mortality ratio	Primary enrolment (gross) M/F	Proportion reaching grade 5 M/F	Secondary enrolment (gross) M/F	% Illiterate (>15 years) M/F	Births per 1,000 women aged 15-19	Contraceptive Prevalence Any method	Contraceptive Prevalence Modern methods	HIV prevalence rate (%) (15-24) M/F
Jamaica	20	73.7 / 77.8	87	100 / 99	87 / 91	82 / 85	17 / 9	79	66	63	0.82 / 0.85
Puerto Rico	10	71.2 / 80.1	19				6 / 6	63	78	68	
Trinidad & Tobago	14	68.4 / 74.4	82	101 / 99	98 / 101	78 / 84	1 / 2	36	53	44	2.45 / 3.25
CENTRAL AMERICA	30	69.5 / 75.4						76	63	55	
Costa Rica	10	75.8 / 80.6	21	108 / 105	77 / 84	58 / 63	5 / 4	78	75	65	0.59 / 0.27
El Salvador	26	67.7 / 73.7	145	112 / 107	69 / 72	50 / 50	18 / 24	87	60	54	0.75 / 0.36
Guatemala	41	63.0 / 68.9	270	106 / 98		39 / 35	24 / 39	111	38	31	0.90 / 0.83
Honduras	32	66.5 / 71.4	108	105 / 107			25 / 25	103	50	41	1.18 / 1.50
Mexico	28	70.4 / 76.4	70	114 / 113	88 / 89	73 / 77	7 / 11	64	67	58	0.37 / 0.09
Nicaragua	36	67.2 / 71.9	233	103 / 104	45 / 53	50 / 58	34 / 33	135	60	57	0.23 / 0.08
Panama	21	72.3 / 77.4	94	113 / 110	92 / 92	67 / 71	7 / 9	89	58	54	1.90 / 1.25
SOUTH AMERICA (15)	32	66.5 / 73.9						71	73	63	
Argentina	20	70.6 / 77.7	75	120 / 120	90 / 90	94 / 100	3 / 3	61			0.85 / 0.34
Bolivia	56	61.8 / 66.0	360	117 / 115	84 / 81	81 / 78	8 / 21	81	53	27	0.11 / 0.06
Brazil	38	64.0 / 72.6	277	166 / 159		103 / 114	13 / 13	73	77	70	0.64 / 0.48
Chile	12	73.0 / 79.0	33	104 / 101	101 / 101	86 / 64	4 / 4	44			0.36 / 0.13
Colombia	26	69.2 / 75.3	92	113 / 112	68 / 73	67 / 73	8 / 8	80	77	64	0.88 / 0.19
Ecuador	41	68.3 / 73.5	185	115 / 115	76 / 79	57 / 58	7 / 10	66	66	50	0.31 / 0.15
Paraguay	37	68.6 / 73.1	106	113 / 110	74 / 79	59 / 61	6 / 8	75	57	48	
Peru	33	67.3 / 72.4	406	128 / 127	88 / 88	83 / 78	5 / 15	55	69	50	0.42 / 0.18
Uruguay	13	71.6 / 78.9	33	110 / 109	93 / 88	92 / 105	3 / 2	70			0.53 / 0.20
Venezuela	19	70.9 / 76.7	89	103 / 101	88 / 94	54 / 65	7 / 8	95	49	38	
NORTHERN AMERICA (16)	7	74.5 / 80.1						50	76	71	
Canada	5	76.7 / 81.9	7	98 / 99		102 / 103		16	75	73	0.28 / 0.18
United States of America	7	74.3 / 79.9	12	101 / 101		95 / 96		53	76	71	0.48 / 0.23
OCEANIA	26	71.8 / 76.6						32	62	58	
AUSTRALIA-NEW ZEALAND	6	76.3 / 81.8						17	76	72	
Australia (17)	6	76.4 / 82.0	7 [9]	102 / 102		160 / 161		16	76	72	0.12 / 0.02
Melanesia (18)	53	59.3 / 61.7						63			
New Zealand	6	75.8 / 80.7	5 [9]	100 / 100		109 / 116		27	75	72	0.05 / 0.02
Papua New Guinea	62	56.8 / 58.7	486	88 / 80		24 / 18	29 / 43	67	26	20	0.33 / 0.39
COUNTRIES WITH ECONOMIES IN TRANSITION OF THE FORMER USSR (19)											
Armenia	17	69.0 / 75.6	51	78 / 79		71 / 76	1 / 2	34	61	22	0.23 / 0.06
Azerbaijan	29	68.7 / 75.5	123	97 / 99		80 / 80		36	55	16	0.06 / 0.02
Belarus	11	64.9 / 75.3	35	109 / 108	71 / 73	83 / 86	0 / 0	27	50	42	0.59 / 0.20
Georgia	18	69.5 / 77.6	89	95 / 96		72 / 74		33	41	20	0.08 / 0.02
Kazakhstan	52	60.9 / 71.9	155	99 / 98		90 / 87	0 / 1	45	66	53	0.13 / 0.03
Kyrgyzstan	37	64.8 / 72.3	113	103 / 100		86 / 86		33	60	49	
Republic of Moldova	18	65.5 / 72.2	46	84 / 84		70 / 72	0 / 2	43	62	43	0.46 / 0.14
Russian Federation	16	60.8 / 73.1	64			80 / 86	0 / 1	30			1.85 / 0.66
Tajikistan	50	66.2 / 71.4	186	108 / 100		86 / 71	0 / 1	25	34	27	
Turkmenistan	49	63.9 / 70.4	128					17	62	53	
Ukraine	14	64.7 / 74.7	39	79 / 77		111 / 99	0 / 1	38	68	38	1.95 / 0.87
Uzbekistan	37	66.8 / 72.5	115				0 / 1	54	67	63	0.01 / <0.01

Demographic, Social and Economic Indicators

	Total population (millions) (2003)	Projected population (millions) (2050)	Ave. pop. growth rate (%) (2000-2005)	% urban (2001)	Urban growth rate (2000-2005)	Population/ ha arable & perm. crop land	Total fertility rate (2000-2005)	% births with skilled atten-dants	GNI per capita PPP$ (2001)	Expen-ditures/ primary student (% of GDP per capita)	Health expen-ditures, public (% of GDP)	External population assistance (US$,000)	Under-5 mortality M/F	Per capita energy con-sumption	Access to safe water
World Total	6,301.5	8,918.7	1.2	48	2.1		2.69					(1,753,151)	81 / 81		
More developed regions (*)	1,203.3	1,219.7	0.2	76	0.4		1.56						10 / 9		
Less developed regions (+)	5,098.2	7,699.1	1.5	41	2.8		2.92						89 / 89		
Least developed countries (‡)	718.1	1,674.5	2.4	26	4.6		5.13						165 / 156		
AFRICA (1)	850.6	1,803.3	2.2	38	3.8		4.91					523,589 [20]	154 / 143		
EASTERN AFRICA	270.3	614.5	2.2	25	4.7		5.61						171 / 156		
Burundi	6.8	19.5	3.1	9	6.4	4.6	6.80	19	590	10.9	1.7	1,146	198 / 178		78
Eritrea	4.1	10.5	3.7	19	6.3	5.7	5.43	21	970	11.1	2.3	3,028	108 / 104		46
Ethiopia	70.7	171.0	2.5	16	4.6	4.8	6.14	10	710	26.5	4.7	31,512	181 / 165	291	23
Kenya	32.0	44.0	1.5	34	4.6	5.1	4.00	44	1,020	0.4	2.7	32,733	125 / 110	515	58
Madagascar	17.4	46.3	2.8	30	4.9	3.4	5.70	46	870	3.9	5.1	7,386	150 / 144		47
Malawi	12.1	25.9	2.0	15	4.6	3.9	6.10	55	620		2.5	25,430	192 / 181		52
Mauritius (2)	1.2	1.5	1.0	42	1.6	1.3	1.95	99	10,410	10.1	3.4	91	21 / 15		100
Mozambique	18.9	31.3	1.8	33	5.1	3.4	5.63	44	1,000		1.3	23,388	223 / 207	403	54
Rwanda	8.4	17.0	2.2	6	4.2	6.0	5.74	31	1,000	6.9	2.7	11,007	189 / 168		41
Somalia	9.9	39.7	4.2	28	5.8	5.9	7.25				0.9		203 / 187		
Uganda	25.8	103.2	3.2	15	5.7	2.6	7.10	38	1,250		1.5	37,434	154 / 139		52
United Republic of Tanzania	37.0	69.1	1.9	33	5.3	5.5	5.11	36	540		2.8	26,995	170 / 153	457	68
Zambia	10.8	18.5	1.2	40	2.7	1.4	5.64	47	790		3.5	28,041	194 / 177	619	64
Zimbabwe	12.9	12.7	0.5	36	3.7	2.4	3.90	73	2,340	13.2	3.1	21,733	118 / 109	809	83
MIDDLE AFRICA (3)	100.6	266.3	2.7	36	4.4		6.28						218 / 196		
Angola	13.6	43.1	3.2	35	4.8	2.9	7.20	23	1,550		2.0	7,015	259 / 234	584	38
Cameroon	16.0	24.9	1.8	50	3.6	1.1	4.61	56	1,670	8.3	1.1	4,541	155 / 142	427	58
Central African Republic	3.9	6.6	1.3	42	2.8	1.3	4.92	44	1,180			764	189 / 157		70
Chad	8.6	25.4	3.0	24	4.7	1.7	6.65	16	930	9.5	1.4	3,044	209 / 192		27
Congo, Democratic Republic of the (4)	52.8	151.6	2.9	31	4.9	4.1	6.70				3.2	3,182	230 / 208	292	45
Congo, Republic of	3.7	10.6	2.6	66	4.0	5.6	6.29		580	9.9	1.1	863	137 / 113	296	53
Gabon	1.3	2.5	1.8	82	3.4	0.9	3.99		5,460	4.6	7.2	435	97 / 87	1,271	87
NORTHERN AFRICA (5)	183.6	306.0	1.9	49	2.7		3.21					72,914 [21]	70 / 61		
Algeria	31.8	48.7	1.7	58	2.7	0.9	2.80	77	5,150		3.0	3,005	52 / 45	956	89
Egypt	71.9	127.4	2.0	43	1.8	7.6	3.29	61	3,790		1.2	55,162	52 / 44	726	97
Libyan Arab Jamahiriya	5.6	9.2	1.9	88	2.5	0.1	3.02	94			3.1	0	23 / 23	3,107	72
Morocco	30.6	47.1	1.6	56	2.9	1.1	2.75	40	3,690	20.5	4.6	7,156	58 / 46	359	80
Sudan	33.6	60.1	2.2	37	4.7	1.2	4.39	86	1,610	45.6	1.0	3,347	131 / 123	521	75
Tunisia	9.8	12.9	1.1	66	2.1	0.5	2.01	90	6,450	16.2		2,528	29 / 24	825	81
SOUTHERN AFRICA	51.7	46.6	0.6	55	2.1		2.79						93 / 83		
Botswana	1.8	1.4	0.9	49	1.4	1.8	3.70	99	8,810		3.8	1,159	108 / 100		95
Lesotho	1.8	1.4	0.1	29	3.4	2.4	3.84	60	2,670	27.0		753	158 / 146		78
Namibia	2.0	2.7	1.4	31	3.3	1.1	4.56	76	6,700	20.7	0.4	3,571	113 / 102	587	77
South Africa	45.0	40.2	0.6	58	2.1	0.4	2.61	84	9,510	14.0	3.7	27,792	85 / 75	2,514	88
Swaziland	1.1	0.9	0.8	27	2.2	1.6	4.54	56	4,690	8.5	3.0	557	155 / 138		
WESTERN AFRICA (6)	244.4	569.9	2.6	40	4.3		5.56						153 / 148		
Benin	6.7	15.6	2.6	43	4.5	1.5	5.66	60	1,030	10.3	1.6	5,390	166 / 146	377	63
Burkina Faso	13.0	42.4	3.0	17	5.1	2.8	6.68	31	1,020		3.0	7,306	165 / 155		42
Côte d'Ivoire	16.6	27.6	1.6	44	3.0	1.1	4.73	47	1,470	14.7	4.4	3,276	182 / 164	433	81
Gambia	1.4	2.9	2.7	31	4.4	4.4	4.70	44	1,730		2.1	801	140 / 128		61

	Total population (millions) (2003)	Projected population (millions) (2050)	Ave. pop. growth rate (%) (2000-2005)	% urban (2001)	Urban growth rate (2000-2005)	Population/ ha arable & perm. crop land	Total fertility rate (2000-2005)	% births with skilled attendants	GNI per capita PPP$ (2001)	Expenditures/ primary student (% of GDP per capita)	Health expenditures, public (% of GDP)	External population assistance (US$,000)	Under-5 mortality M/F	Per capita energy con-sumption	Access to safe water
Ghana	20.9	39.5	2.2	36	3.1	1.9	4.11	44	1,980		8.0	16,997	99 / 88	400	73
Guinea	8.5	19.6	1.6	28	3.1	4.6	5.82	35	1,980	9.5	2.3	6,915	175 / 176		46
Guinea-Bissau	1.5	4.7	2.9	32	4.8	2.8	7.10	25	710		1.9	574	221 / 198		59
Liberia	3.4	9.8	4.0	46	6.8	3.3	6.80				5.2	2,433	238 / 221		
Mali	13.0	46.0	3.0	31	5.1	2.0	7.00	24	810	13.7	6.3	11,804	184 / 178		65
Mauritania	2.9	7.5	3.0	59	5.1	2.8	5.79	40	1,680	11.7	5.8	1,965	163 / 150		36
Niger	12.0	53.0	3.6	21	6.0	2.1	8.00	16	770	22.3	1.8	2,827	207 / 213		59
Nigeria	124.0	258.5	2.5	45	4.4	1.2	5.42	42	830		0.0	39,199	133 / 133	710	62
Senegal	10.1	21.6	2.4	48	4.0	2.9	4.97	51	1,560	13.6	2.6	12,084	116 / 108	324	78
Sierra Leone	5.0	10.3	3.8	37	6.3	5.0	6.50	42	480		2.6	1,120	321 / 293		57
Togo	4.9	10.0	2.3	34	4.2	1.0	5.33	51	1,420	11.6	1.5	1,601	145 / 128	338	54
ASIA	**3,823.4**	**5,222.1**	**1.3**	**38**	**2.7**		**2.55**					**383,548**	**68 / 73**		
EASTERN ASIA (7)	1,512.3	1,590.1	0.7	43	2.6		1.78						36 / 44		
China	1,304.2	1,395.2	0.7	37	3.2	6.3	1.83	70	4,260	6.1	3.1	12,305	39 / 47	905	76
Democratic People's Republic of Korea	22.7	25.0	0.5	61	1.2	3.4	2.02				8.0	354	61 / 55	2,071	100
Hong Kong SAR, China (8)	7.0	9.4	1.1	100	1.2	5.0	1.00		26,050		4.3		5 / 5	2,319	
Japan	127.7	109.7	0.1	79	0.4	1.0	1.32	100	27,430	21.3	2.6	(130,674)[22]	5 / 4	4,136	
Mongolia	2.6	3.8	1.3	57	1.3	0.5	2.42	93	1,800		3.6	2,147	88 / 83		57
Republic of Korea	47.7	46.4	0.6	83	1.3	2.1	1.41	98	18,110	18.3	1.6	0	8 / 6	4,119	92
SOUTH-EASTERN ASIA	543.2	767.2	1.4	38	3.3		2.55						61 / 49		
Cambodia	14.1	29.6	2.4	18	5.5	2.4	4.77	34	1,520	3.2	2.0	16,727	115 / 99		31
Indonesia	219.9	293.8	1.3	42	3.6	2.8	2.35	56	2,940	3.2	0.9	32,589	59 / 46	706	78
Lao People's Democratic Republic	5.7	11.4	2.3	20	4.6	4.2	4.78	21	1,610	6.5	2.2	2,490	144 / 137		35
Malaysia	24.4	39.6	1.9	58	2.9	0.5	2.90	96	8,340	11.2	3.6	206	15 / 11	2,126	39
Myanmar	49.5	64.5	1.3	28	2.9	3.2	2.86	56		1.6	2.7	3,135	137 / 118	262	72
Philippines	80.0	127.0	1.8	59	3.2	3.0	3.18	56	4,360	14.3	1.6	45,132	40 / 30	554	86
Singapore	4.3	4.5	1.7	100	1.7	6.0	1.36				1.3	0	4 / 4	6,120	100
Thailand	62.8	77.1	1.0	20	2.1	1.7	1.93		6,550	12.5	2.1	2,841	31 / 19	1,212	84
Viet Nam	81.4	117.7	1.3	25	3.1	7.2	2.30	70	2,130	7.3	1.3	17,240	52 / 37	471	75
SOUTH CENTRAL ASIA	1,563.2	2,463.9	1.7	30	2.6		3.25						89 / 98		
Afghanistan	23.9	69.5	3.9	22	5.7	1.8	6.80				0.6	1,928	278 / 283		13
Bangladesh	146.7	254.6	2.0	26	4.3	9.0	3.46	13	1,680	7.3	1.4	83,566	85 / 90	142	98
Bhutan	2.3	5.3	3.0	7	5.9	12.2	5.02	15	1,530		3.7	1,431	82 / 78		62
India	1,065.5	1,531.4	1.5	28	2.3	3.2	3.01	42	2,450	7.2	7.5	77,910	78 / 90	494	83
Iran (Islamic Republic of)	68.9	105.5	1.2	65	2.4	1.1	2.33	86	6,230	10.3	0.6	1,539	39 / 39	1,771	93
Nepal	25.2	50.8	2.2	12	5.1	7.2	4.26	12	1,450	14.2	4.2	17,342	91 / 106	343	88
Pakistan	153.6	348.7	2.4	33	3.5	3.3	5.08	20	1,920		0.9	22,992	121 / 135	463	90
Sri Lanka	19.1	21.2	0.8	23	2.4	4.6	2.01	94	3,560		1.8	3,139	30 / 16	437	76
WESTERN ASIA	204.7	400.8	2.1	65	2.5		3.45					47,102	60 / 53		
Iraq	25.2	57.9	2.7	67	2.7	0.4	4.77	54			2.6	326	112 / 103	1,190	80
Israel	6.4	10.0	2.0	92	2.2	0.4	2.70	99		21.2	5.1	0	9 / 9	3,241	
Jordan	5.5	10.2	2.7	79	3.0	1.4	3.57	97	4,080	13.7	6.0	11,570	28 / 26	1,061	97
Kuwait	2.5	4.9	3.5	96	2.6	2.1	2.66	98			2.7	9	13 / 13	10,529	
Lebanon	3.7	4.9	1.6	90	1.9	0.4	2.18	89	4,640	10.5	1.9	1,902	22 / 17	1,169	100
Occupied Palestinian Territory	3.6	11.1	3.6	67	4.1		5.57	97				4,772	27 / 21		93
Oman	2.9	6.8	2.9	77	4.0	11.4	4.96	91		11.4	2.3	17,739	26 / 20	4,046	38

Demographic, Social and Economic Indicators

	Total population (millions) (2003)	Projected population (millions) (2050)	Ave. pop. growth rate (%) (2000-2005)	% urban (2001)	Urban growth rate (2000-2005)	Population/ha arable & perm. crop land	Total fertility rate (2000-2005)	% births with skilled attendants	GNI per capita PPP$ (2001)	Expenditures/primary student (% of GDP per capita)	Health expenditures, public (% of GDP)	External population assistance (US$,000)	Under-5 mortality M/F	Per capita energy consumption	Access to safe water
Saudi Arabia	24.2	54.7	2.9	87	3.6	0.5	4.53	91			4.2	0	26 / 23	5,081	95
Syrian Arab Republic	17.8	34.2	2.4	52	3.3	0.8	3.32	76	3,440	12.9	1.6	840	28 / 25	1,137	80
Turkey (10)	71.3	97.8	1.4	66	1.9	0.8	2.43	81	6,640	17.6	3.6	2,799	56 / 43	1,181	83
United Arab Emirates	3.0	4.1	1.9	87	2.2	0.5	2.82	96		8.5	2.5	8	17 / 14	10,175	
Yemen	20.0	84.4	3.5	25	5.3	5.6	7.01	22	770			7,136	100 / 95	201	70
EUROPE	**726.3**	**631.9**	**-0.1**	**74**	**0.3**		**1.38**						**12 / 10**		
EASTERN EUROPE	**300.3**	**221.7**	**-0.5**	**68**	**-0.5**		**1.18**					**21,809**[21,23]	**20 / 16**		
Bulgaria	7.9	5.3	-0.8	70	-0.9	0.1	1.10		5,950	15.2	3.0	74	21 / 17	2,299	100
Czech Republic	10.2	8.6	-0.1	67	0.0	0.3	1.16	99	14,550	12.5	4.3	0	6 / 6	3,931	
Hungary	9.9	7.6	-0.5	65	-0.1	0.2	1.20		12,570	17.7		0	12 / 10	2,448	99
Poland	38.6	33.0	-0.1	63	0.3	0.5	1.26	99	9,280	26.5	4.2	113	11 / 10	2,328	
Romania	22.3	18.1	-0.2	55	0.1	0.3	1.32	99	6,980	19.9	1.9	1,697	28 / 22	1,619	57
Slovakia	5.4	4.9	0.1	58	0.4	0.3	1.28		11,610	10.8	5.3	0	10 / 10	3,234	100
NORTHERN EUROPE (11)	**94.8**	**100.1**	**0.2**	**84**	**0.2**		**1.61**						**7 / 6**		
Denmark	5.4	5.3	0.2	85	0.2	0.1	1.77	100	27,950	23.4	6.6	(4,460)	7 / 6	3,643	
Estonia	1.3	0.7	-1.1	69	-1.1	0.1	1.22		10,020	24.5	2.8	67	13 / 9	3,303	
Finland	5.2	4.9	0.1	59	0.1	0.1	1.73	100	25,180	17.3	2.5	(19,766)	5 / 4	6,409	100
Ireland	4.0	5.0	1.1	59	1.4	0.4	1.90	100	27,460	13.3	2.2	(4,240)	7 / 7	3,854	
Latvia	2.3	1.3	-0.9	60	-0.6	0.2	1.10	100	7,870	23.6	3.3	51	19 / 16	1,541	
Lithuania	3.4	2.5	-0.6	69	0.0	0.2	1.25		7,610	61.4	1.6	48	13 / 10	2,032	
Norway	4.5	4.9	0.4	75	0.7	0.3	1.80	100	30,440	29.2	6.7	(59,957)	6 / 5	5,704	
Sweden	8.9	8.7	0.1	83	-0.1	0.1	1.64	100	24,670	23.5	6.5	(73,142)	5 / 4	5,354	100
United Kingdom	59.3	66.2	0.3	90	0.3	0.2	1.60		24,460	14.0	5.9	(169,602)	7 / 6	3,962	
SOUTHERN EUROPE (12)	**146.4**	**125.6**	**0.1**	**67**	**0.4**		**1.32**						**10 / 9**		
Albania	3.2	3.7	0.7	43	2.1	2.2	2.28		3,880		2.1	1,363	37 / 31	521	97
Bosnia & Herzegovina	4.2	3.6	1.1	43	2.2	0.3	1.30	100			3.1	189	17 / 14	1,096	
Croatia	4.4	3.6	-0.2	58	0.8	0.2	1.65	100	8,440		1.0	0	10 / 8	1,775	
Greece	11.0	9.8	0.1	60	0.5	0.4	1.27		17,860	16.0	2.3		8 / 7	2,635	
Italy	57.4	44.9	-0.1	67	0.1	0.3	1.23		24,340	21.2	8.3	(24,921)	7 / 6	2,974	
Macedonia (Former Yugoslav Republic of)	2.1	2.2	0.5	59	0.4	0.4	1.90	97	4,860		5.3		19 / 18		
Portugal	10.1	9.0	0.1	66	1.9	0.5	1.45	98	17,270	20.5	5.8	(400)	9 / 8	2,459	
Serbia and Montenegro	10.5	9.4	-0.1	52	0.2	0.6	1.65	99			2.9	3,478	17 / 14	1,289	98
Slovenia	2.0	1.6	-0.1	49	-0.1	0.2	1.14	100	18,160		6.8	0	8 / 7	3,288	
Spain	41.1	37.3	0.2	78	0.3	0.2	1.15		20,150	18.8	5.4	(6,208)	7 / 6	3,084	
WESTERN EUROPE (13)	**184.9**	**184.5**	**0.2**	**83**	**0.3**		**1.58**						**6 / 6**		
Austria	8.1	7.4	0.0	67	0.2	0.3	1.28	100	27,080	25.1	5.6	(870)	6 / 5	3,524	100
Belgium	10.3	10.2	0.2	97	0.2	0.2[24]	1.66	100	28,210	17.0	6.2	(15,768)	6 / 6	5,776	
France	60.1	64.2	0.5	76	0.6	0.1	1.89	99	25,280	18.0	5.0	(12,360)	6 / 6	4,366	
Germany	82.5	79.1	0.1	88	0.2	0.2	1.35	100	25,530	17.8	0.8	(96,398)[25]	6 / 6	4,131	
Netherlands	16.1	17.0	0.5	90	0.5	0.6	1.72	100	26,440	15.4	0.9	(170,077)	7 / 6	4,762	100
Switzerland	7.2	5.8	0.0	68		1.1	1.41		31,320	23.2	6.0	(16,074)	7 / 5	3,704	100
LATIN AMERICA & CARIBBEAN	**543.2**	**767.7**	**1.4**	**76**	**1.9**		**2.53**					**155,279**	**45 / 36**		
CARIBBEAN (14)	**38.7**	**45.8**	**0.9**	**63**	**1.6**		**2.39**						**62 / 53**		
Cuba	11.3	10.1	0.3	76	0.5	0.4	1.55	100		34.7	8.0	455	12 / 8	1,180	91
Dominican Republic	8.7	11.9	1.5	66	2.4	0.9	2.71	99	5,870		4.3	6,742	58 / 48	932	86
Haiti	8.3	12.4	1.3	36	3.3	5.6	3.98	27	1,450		4.2	11,419	119 / 104	256	58

	Total population (millions) (2003)	Projected population (millions) (2050)	Ave. pop. growth rate (%) (2000-2005)	% urban (2001)	Urban growth rate (2000-2005)	Population/ ha arable & perm. crop land	Total fertility rate (2000-2005)	% births with skilled atten-dants	GNI per capita PPP$ (2001)	Expen-ditures/ primary student (% of GDP per capita)	Health expen-ditures, public (% of GDP)	External population assistance (US$,000)	Under-5 mortality M/F	Per capita energy con-sumption	Access to safe water
Jamaica	2.7	3.7	0.9	57	1.8	1.9	2.36	95	3,650	16.2	6.0	5,066	28 / 21	1,524	92
Puerto Rico	3.9	3.7	0.5	76	1.3	1.4	1.89					0	14 / 11		
Trinidad & Tobago	1.3	1.2	0.3	75	1.0	0.9	1.55	99	9,080	16.2	2.6	331	21 / 16	6,660	
CENTRAL AMERICA	142.3	211.8	1.7	69	2.0		2.76						41 / 34		
Costa Rica	4.2	6.5	1.9	60	2.9	1.7	2.28	98	8,080	14.9	1.5	419	14 / 11	861	96
El Salvador	6.5	9.8	1.6	62	3.5	2.6	2.88	90	4,500	2.0	1.8	5,057	38 / 31	651	81
Guatemala	12.3	26.2	2.6	40	3.4	3.0	4.41	41	3,850	4.9	3.4	7,578	58 / 51	628	92
Honduras	6.9	12.6	2.3	54	4.0	1.6	3.72	55	2,450		6.0	12,998	53 / 43	469	89
Mexico	103.5	140.2	1.5	75	1.7	0.9	2.50	86	8,770	11.7	1.9	16,214	37 / 31	1,567	88
Nicaragua	5.5	10.9	2.4	57	3.3	0.4	3.75	65		20.5	2.3	11,888	50 / 40	542	77
Panama	3.1	5.1	1.8	57	2.0	1.0	2.70	90	5,720	15.8	5.3	318	31 / 23	892	90
SOUTH AMERICA (15)	362.3	510.1	1.4	80	1.9		2.45						45 / 35		
Argentina	38.4	52.8	1.2	88	1.4	0.1	2.44	98	11,690	12.5	4.7	1,045	26 / 21	1,660	94
Bolivia	8.8	15.7	1.9	63	3.0	1.6	3.82	59	2,380	13.3	4.9	16,682	77 / 67	592	83
Brazil	178.5	233.1	1.2	82	1.9	0.4	2.21	92	7,450	12.5	3.4	10,602	52 / 39	1,077	87
Chile	15.8	21.8	1.2	86	1.5	1.1	2.35	100	9,420	13.9	2.5	108	15 / 12	1,604	93
Colombia	44.2	67.5	1.6	76	2.3	1.9	2.62	86	5,984		1.9	1,259	35 / 30	681	92
Ecuador	13.0	18.7	1.5	63	2.4	1.2	2.76	99	3,070	4.3	1.8	6,600	60 / 49	647	85
Paraguay	5.9	12.1	2.4	57	3.6	0.9	3.84	71	4,400	10.9	3.0	2,201	51 / 39	715	78
Peru	27.2	41.1	1.5	73	2.1	1.8	2.86	56	4,680	8.0	2.8	20,085	57 / 47	489	80
Uruguay	3.4	4.1	0.7	92	0.9	0.3	2.30	100	8,710	8.2	5.1	107	18 / 13	923	98
Venezuela	25.7	41.7	1.9	87	2.1	0.7	2.72	95	5,890		2.7	459	25 / 20	2,452	83
NORTHERN AMERICA (16)	325.7	447.9	1.0	78	1.2		2.05						8 / 8		
Canada	31.5	39.1	0.8	79	1.1	0.0	1.48	100	27,870		6.6	(37,441)	7 / 6	8,156	100
United States of America	294.0	408.7	1.0	77	1.2	0.0	2.11	99	34,870	17.9	5.8	(658,614)	8 / 9	8,148	100
OCEANIA	32.2	45.8	1.2	74	1.5		2.34						34 / 35		
AUSTRALIA-NEW ZEALAND	23.6	30.1	0.9	90	1.3		1.75						8 / 6		
Australia (17)	19.7	25.6	1.0	91	1.4	0.0	1.70	100	25,780	15.9	6.0	(14,673)	8 / 6	5,744	100
Melanesia (18)	7.5	14.0	2.1	24	3.5		3.91						70 / 75		
New Zealand	3.9	4.5	0.8	86	0.9	0.1	2.01	95	19,130	19.9	6.2	(2,308)	8 / 6	4,864	
Papua New Guinea	5.7	11.1	2.2	18	3.7	4.3	4.09	53	2,150	11.1	3.6	6,955	81 / 88		42
COUNTRIES WITH ECONOMIES IN TRANSITION OF THE FORMER USSR (19)															
Armenia	3.1	2.3	-0.5	67	0.2	0.9	1.15	97	2,880	4.0	3.2	1,876	22 / 17	542	
Azerbaijan	8.4	10.9	0.9	52	0.6	1.1	2.10	88	3,020	24.8	0.7	1,473	41 / 38	1,454	76
Belarus	9.9	7.5	-0.5	70	-0.2	0.2	1.20	100	8,030		4.7	19	17 / 12	2,432	100
Georgia	5.1	3.5	-0.9	57	-0.1	1.0	1.40	96	2,860		3.4	1,448	25 / 18	533	77
Kazakhstan	15.4	13.9	-0.4	56	-0.3	0.1	1.95	99	6,370		4.2	3,047	68 / 48	2,594	91
Kyrgyzstan	5.1	7.2	1.4	34	1.2	0.9	2.64	98	2,710		2.6	1,518	50 / 42	497	77
Republic of Moldova	4.3	3.6	-0.1	41	0.0	0.4	1.40		2,420	1.3	3.0	1,514	26 / 21	671	92
Russian Federation	143.2	101.5	-0.6	73	-0.6	0.1	1.14	99	8,660		3.8	6,369	23 / 18	4,218	99
Tajikistan	6.2	9.6	0.9	28	0.7	2.4	3.06	71	1,150		1.0	369	78 / 67	470	60
Turkmenistan	4.9	7.5	1.5	45	2.3	0.9	2.70	97	4,580		4.6	684	74 / 61	2,627	
Ukraine	48.5	31.7	-0.8	68	-0.8	0.2	1.15	100	4,150		2.9	2,436	20 / 15	2,820	98
Uzbekistan	26.1	37.8	1.5	37	1.4	1.4	2.44	96	2,470		2.6	1,444	56 / 48	2,027	89

Selected Indicators for Less Populous Countries/Territories

Monitoring ICPD Goals – Selected Indicators	Indicators of Mortality			Indicators of Education		Reproductive Health Indicators			
	Infant mortality Total per 1,000 live births	Life expectancy M/F	Maternal mortality ratio	Primary enrolment (gross) M/F	Secondary enrolment (gross) M/F	Births per 1,000 women aged 15-19	Contraceptive Prevalence Any method	Modern methods	HIV prevalence rate (%) (15-24) M/F
Bahamas	18	63.9 / 70.3	34	92 / 89	85 / 83	60	62	60	2.65 / 3.05
Bahrain	14	72.5 / 75.9	69	103 / 103	98 / 105	18	62	31	
Barbados	11	74.5 / 79.5	0	110 / 110	101 / 102	43	55	53	
Belize	31	69.9 / 73.0	139	130 / 126	71 / 77	86	47	42	1.09 / 2.00
Brunei Darussalam	6	74.2 / 78.9	32	106 / 102	109 / 116	26			
Cape Verde	30	67.0 / 72.8	96	140 / 137		82	53	46	
Comoros	67	59.4 / 62.2	547	92 / 80	23 / 18	59	21	11	
Cyprus	8	76.0 / 80.5	0	97 / 97	93 / 94	10			
Djibouti	102	44.7 / 46.8	774	46 / 35	13 / 17	64			
Equatorial Guinea	101	47.8 / 50.5	774	126 / 115	43 / 19	192			1.41 / 2.75
Fiji	18	68.1 / 71.5	99	111 / 110		54	41	35	
French Polynesia	9	70.7 / 75.8	20			45			
Guadaloupe	7	74.8 / 81.7	5			19	44	31	
Guam	10	72.4 / 77.0	12			70			
Guyana	51	60.1 / 66.3	167	122 / 118		67	31	28	3.25 / 4.00
Iceland	3	77.6 /81.9	10	102 / 102	105 / 113	19			
Luxembourg	5	75.1 / 81.4	24	101 / 101	92 / 97	9			
Maldives	38	67.8 / 67.0	153	131 / 131	53 / 57	53			
Malta	7	75.9 / 80.7	0	106 / 107	89 / 89	12			
Martinique	7	75.8 / 82.3	4			30	51	38	
Micronesia (26)	21	70.3 / 74.0				53			
Netherlands Antilles	13	73.3 / 79.2	20	119 / 103	88 / 99	44			
New Caledonia	7	72.5 / 77.7	10			31			
Polynesia (27)	21	68.9 / 73.4				39			
Qatar	12	70.5 / 75.4	15	105 / 104	86 / 92	20	43	32	
Réunion	8	71.2 / 79.3	78			32	67	62	
Samoa	26	66.9 / 73.4	15	105 / 101	73 / 79	44			
Solomon Islands	21	67.9 / 70.7	97			52			
Suriname	26	68.5 / 73.7	112	127 / 126	80 / 94	42			1.20 / 1.50
Timor-Leste, Democratic Republic of	124	48.7 / 50.4	630			27			
Vanuatu	29	67.5 / 70.5	32	113 / 121	31 / 26	52			

Demographic, Social and Economic Indicators	Total population (thousands) (2003)	Projected population (thousands) (2050)	% urban (2001)	Urban growth rate (2000-2005)	Population/ ha arable & perm. crop land	Total fertility rate (2000-2005)	% births with skilled attendants	GNI per capita PPP$ (2001)	Under-5 mortality M/F
Bahamas	314	395	88.9	1.6	1.0	2.29			27 / 21
Bahrain	724	1,270	92.5	2.0	1.2	2.66	98		20 / 16
Barbados	270	258	50.5	1.4	0.6	1.50	91		13 / 11
Belize	256	421	48.1	2.2	0.8	3.15	77	5,350	43 / 42
Brunei Darussalam	358	685	72.8	2.5	0.4	2.48	98		8 / 6
Cape Verde	463	812	63.5	3.9	2.4	3.30	89	4,870	45 / 26
Comoros	768	1,816	33.8	4.6	4.1	4.90	62	1,610	96 / 87
Cyprus	802	892	70.2	1.2	0.5	1.90	100		8 / 8
Djibouti	703	1,395	84.2	1.3		5.70		2,120	185 / 168
Equatorial Guinea	494	1,177	49.3	4.9	1.4	5.89	5	5,640	181 / 164
Fiji	839	969	50.2	2.5	1.1	2.88		5,140	21 / 23
French Polynesia	244	355	52.6	1.6		2.44			11 / 11
Guadaloupe	440	467	99.6	0.8	0.6	2.10			11 / 8
Guam	163	248	39.5	3.0		2.88			13 / 10
Guyana	765	507	36.7	1.4	0.3	2.31		3,750	81 / 60
Iceland	290	330	92.7	0.8	3.3	1.95		29,830	5 / 4
Luxembourg	453	716	91.9	1.6	0.2[24]	1.73	100	48,080	7 / 7
Maldives	318	819	28.0	4.6	26.3	5.33	90	4,520	41 / 56
Malta	394	402	91.2	0.7	0.7	1.77	98		9 / 8
Martinique	393	413	95.2	0.8	0.8	1.90			9 / 8
Micronesia (26)	526	863	28.6	3.6		3.40			26 / 25
Netherlands Antilles	221	249	69.3	1.1	0.1	2.05			17 / 11
New Caledonia	228	382	78.1	3.2		2.45			9 / 10
Polynesia (27)	635	912	40.4	1.9		3.16			26 / 26
Qatar	610	874	92.9	1.7	0.3	3.22	98		17 / 13
Réunion	756	1,014	72.1	2.2	0.6	2.30			11 / 9
Samoa	178	254	22.3	1.4		4.12	76	5,450	34 / 29
Solomon Islands	477	1,071	20.2	6.0	5.5	4.42	85	1,680	31 / 30
Suriname	436	459	74.8	1.3	1.2	2.45	95	3,310	35 / 23
Timor-Leste, Democratic Republic of	778	1,433	7.5	4.7	7.6	3.85			186 / 179
Vanuatu	212	435	22.1	4.2		4.13	87	2,710	32 / 39

Notes for Indicators

The designations employed in this publication do not imply the expression of any opinion on the part of the United Nations Population Fund concerning the legal status of any country, territory or area or of its authorities, or concerning the delimitation of its frontiers or boundaries.

Data for small countries or areas, generally those with population of 200,000 or less in 1990, are not given in this table separately. They have been included in their regional population figures.

(*) More-developed regions comprise North America, Japan, Europe and Australia-New Zealand.

(+) Less-developed regions comprise all regions of Africa, Latin America and Caribbean, Asia (excluding Japan), and Melanesia, Micronesia and Polynesia.

(‡) Least-developed countries according to standard United Nations designation.

(1) Including British Indian Ocean Territory and Seychelles.

(2) Including Agalesa, Rodrigues and St. Brandon.

(3) Including Sao Tome and Principe.

(4) Formerly Zaire.

(5) Including Western Sahara.

(6) Including St. Helena, Ascension and Tristan da Cunha.

(7) Including Macau.

(8) On 1 July 1997, Hong Kong became a Special Administrative Region (SAR) of China.

(9) This entry is included in the more developed regions aggregate but not in the estimate for the geographical region.

(10) Turkey is included in Western Asia for geographical reasons. Other classifications include this country in Europe.

(11) Including Channel Islands, Faeroe Islands and Isle of Man.

(12) Including Andorra, Gibraltar, Holy See and San Marino.

(13) Including Leichtenstein and Monaco.

(14) Including Anguilla, Antigua and Barbuda, Aruba, British Virgin Islands, Cayman Islands, Dominica, Grenada, Montserrat, Netherlands Antilles, Saint Kitts and Nevis, Saint Lucia, Saint Vincent and the Grenadines, Turks and Caicos Islands, and United States Virgin Islands.

(15) Including Falkland Islands (Malvinas) and French Guiana.

(16) Including Bermuda, Greenland, and St. Pierre and Miquelon.

(17) Including Christmas Island, Cocos (Keeling) Islands and Norfolk Island.

(18) Including New Caledonia and Vanuatu.

(19) The successor States of the former USSR are grouped under existing regions. Eastern Europe includes Belarus, Republic of Moldova, Russian Federation and Ukraine. Western Asia includes Armenia, Azerbaijan and Georgia. South Central Asia includes Kazakhstan, Kyrgyzstan, Tajikistan, Turkmenistan and Uzbekistan. Regional total, excluding subregion reported separately below.

(20) Regional total, excluding subregion reported separately below.

(21) These subregions are included in the UNFPA Arab States and Europe region.

(22) Estimates based on previous years' reports. Updated data are expected.

(23) Total for Eastern Europe includes some South European Balkan States and Northern European Baltic States.

(24) This figure includes Belgium and Luxembourg.

(25) More recent reports suggest this figure might have been higher. Future publications will reflect the evaluation of this information.

(26) Comprising Federated States of Micronesia, Guam, Kiribati, Marshall Islands, Nauru, Northern Mariana Islands, and Pacific Islands (Palau).

(27) Comprising American Samoa, Cook Islands, Johnston Island, Pitcairn, Samoa, Tokelau, Tonga, Midway Islands, Tuvalu, and Wallis and Futuna Islands.

Technical Notes

The statistical tables in this year's *State of World Population* report once again give special attention to indicators that can help track progress in meeting the quantitative and qualitative goals of the International Conference on Population and Development (ICPD) and the Millennium Development Goals (MDGs) in the areas of mortality reduction, access to education, access to reproductive health services including family planning and HIV/AIDS prevalence among young people. Several changes have been made in other indicators, as noted below. Future reports will include different process measures when these become available, as ICPD and MDG follow-up efforts lead to improved monitoring systems. Improved monitoring of the financial contributions of governments, non-governmental organizations and the private sector should also allow better future reporting of expenditures and resource mobilization for ICPD/MDG implementation efforts. The sources for the indicators and their rationale for selection follow, by category.

Monitoring ICPD goals

INDICATORS OF MORTALITY

Infant mortality, male and female life expectancy at birth. Source: United Nations Population Division. 2003. *World Population Prospects: The 2002 Revision.* New York: United Nations. Spreadsheets provided by the United Nations Population Division. These indicators are measures of mortality levels, respectively, in the first year of life (which is most sensitive to development levels) and over the entire lifespan.

    Maternal mortality ratio. Source: "Maternal Mortality in 2000: Estimates Developed by WHO, UNICEF and UNFPA" (forthcoming). This indicator presents the number of deaths to women per 100,000 live births which result from conditions related to pregnancy, delivery and related complications. Precision is difficult, though relative magnitudes are informative. Estimates below 50 are not rounded; those 50-100 are rounded to the nearest 5; 100-1,000, to the nearest 10; and above 1,000, to the nearest 100. Several of the estimates differ from official government figures. The estimates are based on reported figures wherever possible, using approaches to improve the comparability of information from different sources. See the source for details on the origin of particular national estimates. Estimates and methodologies are regularly reviewed by WHO, UNICEF, UNFPA, academic institutions

and other agencies and are revised where necessary as part of the ongoing process of improving maternal mortality data. Because of changes in methods, prior estimates for 1995 levels may not be strictly comparable with these estimates.

INDICATORS OF EDUCATION

Male and female gross primary enrolment ratios, male and female gross secondary enrolment ratios. Source: Spreadsheets provided by UNESCO Institute for Statistics, Montreal. Gross enrolment ratios indicate the number of students enrolled in a level in the education system per 100 individuals in the appropriate age group. They do not correct for individuals who are older than the level-appropriate age due to late starts, interrupted schooling or grade repetition.

    Male and female adult illiteracy. Source: Spreadsheets provided by UNESCO Institute for Statistics, Montreal. Illiteracy definitions are subject to variation in different countries; three widely accepted definitions are in use. In so far as possible, data refer to the proportion who cannot, with understanding, both read and write a short simple statement on everyday life. Adult illiteracy (rates for persons above 15 years of age) reflects both recent levels of educational enrolment and past educational attainment. The above education indicators have been updated using the UN Population Division estimates from *World Population Prospects (The 2000 Revision).* New York: United Nations. Education data are for the most recent year estimates available for the 1998-2000 period.

    Proportion reaching grade 5 of primary education. Source: UNESCO Institute for Statistics spreadsheet: School Life Expectancy, Percentage of Repeaters and Survival Rate in Primary Education by Country and Gender. Data are most recent within the years 1998-2000. Thirteen countries reported data to grade 4 (see original source).

INDICATORS OF REPRODUCTIVE HEALTH

Births per 1,000 women aged 15-19. Source: Spreadsheets provided by the United Nations Population Division. This is an indicator of the burden of fertility on young women. Since it is an annual level summed over all women in the age cohort, it does not reflect fully the level of fertility for women during their youth. Since it indicates the annual average number of births per woman per year, one could multiply it by five to approximate the number of births to 1,000 young women during their late teen years.

The measure does not indicate the full dimensions of teen pregnancy as only live births are included in the numerator. Stillbirths and spontaneous or induced abortions are not reflected.

Contraceptive prevalence. Source: United Nations Population Division. 2003. *Database on Contraceptive Use* (updated June 2003). New York: United Nations. These data are derived from sample survey reports and estimate the proportion of married women (including women in consensual unions) currently using, respectively, any method or modern methods of contraception. Modern or clinic and supply methods include male and female sterilization, IUD, the pill, injectables, hormonal implants, condoms and female barrier methods. These numbers are roughly but not completely comparable across countries due to variation in the timing of the surveys and in the details of the questions. Unlike in past years, all country and regional data refer to women aged 15-49. All of the data were collected in 1995 or later. The most recent survey data available are cited.

HIV prevalence rate, M/F, 15-24. Source: UNAIDS. 2002. *The Report on the Global HIV/AIDS Epidemic*. Geneva: UNAIDS. These data derive from surveillance system reports and model estimates. Data provided for men and women aged 15-24 are, respectively, averages of high and low estimates for each country. The reference year is 2001. Male-female differences reflect physiological and social vulnerability to the illness and are affected by age differences between sexual partners.

Demographic, Social and Economic Indicators

Total population 2003, projected population 2050, average annual population growth rate for 2000-2005. Source: Spreadsheets provided by the United Nations Population Division. These indicators present the size, projected future size and current period annual growth of national populations.

Per cent urban, urban growth rates. Source: United Nations Population Division. 2002. *World Urbanization Prospects: The 2001 Revision: Data Tables and Highlights* (Doc. ESA/P/WP.173.) New York: United Nations. These indicators reflect the proportion of the national population living in urban areas and the growth rate in urban areas projected for 2000-2005.

Agricultural population per hectare of arable and permanent crop land. Source: Data provided by Food and Agriculture Organization (from FAO Statistical Development Service), using agricultural population data based on the total populations from United Nations Population Division. 2001. *World Population Prospects: The 2000 Revision*. New York: United Nations. This indicator relates the size of the agricultural population to the land suitable for agricultural production. It is responsive to changes in both the structure of national economies (proportions of the workforce in agriculture) and in technologies for land development. High values can be related to stress on land productivity and to fragmentation of land holdings. However, the measure is also sensitive to differing development levels and land use policies. Data refer to the year 2000.

Total fertility rate (period: 2000-2005). Source: Spreadsheets provided by the United Nations Population Division. The measure indicates the number of children a woman would have during her reproductive years if she bore children at the rate estimated for different age groups in the specified time period. Countries may reach the projected level at different points within the period.

Births with skilled attendants. Source: UNICEF Global Database: Skilled Attendant at Delivery (on UNICEF web site). Data for more developed countries are not available. This indicator is based on national reports of the proportion of births attended by "skilled health personnel or skilled attendant: doctors (specialist or non-specialist) and/or persons with midwifery skills who can diagnose and manage obstetrical complications as well as normal deliveries". Data for more developed countries reflect their higher levels of skilled delivery attendance. Because of assumptions of full coverage, data (and coverage) deficits of marginalized populations and the impacts of chance and transport delays may not be fully reflected in official statistics. Data estimates are the most recent available.

Gross national income per capita. Source: 2001 figures from: The World Bank. *World Development Indicators* Online. Washington, D.C.: The World Bank. This indicator (formerly referred to as gross national product [GNP] per capita) measures the total output of goods and services for final use produced by residents and non-residents, regardless of allocation to domestic and foreign claims, in relation to the size of the population. As such, it is an indicator of the economic productivity of a nation. It differs from gross domestic product (GDP) by further adjusting for income received from abroad for labour and capital by residents, for similar payments to non-residents, and by incorporating various technical adjustments including those related to exchange rate changes over time. This measure also takes into account the differing purchasing power of currencies by including purchasing power parity (PPP) adjustments of "real GNI". Some PPP figures are based on regression models; others are extrapolated from the latest International Comparison Programme benchmark estimates; see original source for details.

Central government expenditures on education and health. Source: The World Bank. 2003. *World Development Indicators Online.* Washington, D.C.: The World Bank. These indicators reflect the priority afforded to education and health sectors by a country through the government expenditures dedicated to them. They are not sensitive to differences in allocations within sectors, e.g., primary education or health services in relation to other levels, which vary considerably. Direct comparability is complicated by the different administrative and budgetary responsibilities allocated to central governments in relation to local governments, and to the varying roles of the private and public sectors. Reported estimates are presented as shares of GDP per capita (for education) or total GDP (for health). Great caution is also advised about cross-country comparisons because of varying costs of inputs in different settings and sectors. Data refer to the most recent estimates 1998-2001.

External assistance for population. Source: UNFPA. 2002. *Financial Resource Flows for Population Activities in 2000.* New York: UNFPA. This figure provides the amount of external assistance expended in 2000 for population activities in each country. External funds are disbursed through multilateral and bilateral assistance agencies and by non-governmental organizations. Donor countries are indicated by their contributions being placed in parentheses. Future editions of this report will use other indicators to provide a better basis for comparing and evaluating resource flows in support of population and reproductive health programmes from various national and international sources. Regional totals include both country-level projects and regional activities (not otherwise reported in the table).

Under-5 mortality. Source: United Nations Population Division, special tabulation based on: United Nations. 2003. *World Population Prospects: The 2002 Revision.* New York: United Nations. This indicator relates to the incidence of mortality to infants and young children. It reflects, therefore, the impact of diseases and other causes of death on infants, toddlers and young children. More standard demographic measures are infant mortality and mortality rates for 1 to 4 years of age, which reflect differing causes of and frequency of mortality in these ages. The measure is more sensitive than infant mortality to the burden of childhood diseases, including those preventable by improved nutrition and by immunization programmes. Under-5 mortality is here expressed as deaths to children under 5 per 1,000 live births in a given year. The estimate refers to the period 2000-2005.

Per capita energy consumption. Source: The World Bank. 2003. *World Development Indicators* Online. Washington, D.C.: The World Bank. This indicator reflects annual consumption of commercial primary energy (coal, lignite, petroleum, natural gas and hydro, nuclear and geothermal electricity) in kilograms of oil equivalent per capita. It reflects the level of industrial development, the structure of the economy and patterns of consumption. Changes over time can reflect changes in the level and balance of various economic activities and changes in the efficiency of energy use (including decreases or increases in wasteful consumption). Data are for 2000.

Access to safe water. Source: Calculations from rural and urban improved water source data provided in UNICEF End-decade Databases: Water and per cent urban data from the United Nations Population Division (see above). This indicator reports the percentage of the population with access to an adequate amount of safe drinking water located within a *convenient distance* from the user's dwelling. The italicized words use country-level definitions. The indicator is related to exposure to health risks, including those resulting from improper sanitation. Data are estimates for the year 2000.

Editorial Team

The State of World Population 2003

Editors: Stan Bernstein and William A. Ryan
Editorial Assistant: Phyllis Brachman
Editorial Research: Ann Erb-Leoncavallo, Margaret E. Greene,
Karen Hardee, Don Hinrichsen, Janet Jensen, Mia MacDonald,
Alex Marshall, Judith Senderowitz, Micol Zarb
Intern: Jeni Incontro

Prepress/Production: Prographics, Inc., Annapolis, Maryland, USA

Photo captions and credits

Front cover
© William A. Ryan/UNFPA
Afghanistan, July 2003. Student at newly opened girls' school run by the Afghan Institute of Learning learns income-earning skills.

Contents page
© Jonathan Silvers
Since losing both parents to AIDS in 1999, Sarah, 15, has struggled to raise her younger brother and sister in northern Zambia. She attends school only a few hours each week.

Chapter 1
© Jonathan Silvers
Yasmin, 16, left school in third grade. She has spent half her life selling flowers on the streets of Dhaka, Bangladesh.

Chapter 2
© Mark Edwards/Still Pictures
Sex education class for girls in a village in Haryana State, India.

Chapter 3
© Jorgen Schytte/Still Pictures
Schoolchildren in Uganda learn about HIV/AIDS.

Chapter 4
© Rick Maiman
David and Lucile Packard Foundation
Young people in Mexico.

Chapter 5
© Mark Edwards/Still Pictures
Gaborone, Botswana. Teenage mothers with their babies.

Chapter 6
© Ian Berry/Magnum Photos
Tunisian students gather outside after a lesson in computing.

Chapter 7
© Jorgen Schytte/Still Pictures
Teenage boys in Zomba City, Malawi.

Page 60
© Steve McCurry/Magnum Photos
Village guide in Niamey, Niger.

United Nations Population Fund
220 East 42nd Street, 23rd Flr.
New York, NY 10017 U.S.A.
www.unfpa.org